D1794946

A Britespot Publication

KEVIN
RATCLIFFE

My Memories of Everton

Howard Kendall, easily the best manager that I've worked with

FOREWORD
By Howard Kendall

A good atmosphere in the dressing room is a key ingredient in building a winning team and Kevin Ratcliffe helped to develop a wonderful team spirit at Goodison Park and at the Bellefield Training ground.

The players respected Kevin as their captain and although he never let them step out of line, he was the catalyst in creating a wonderful camaraderie in the squad both on the field and off it.

As a captain, Kevin led by example and his incredible pace gave a new dimension to the Everton defensive line-up where he dominated the centre of the park in almost every game he played.

It is perhaps no coincidence that during his time at the club, Everton enjoyed their most successful time in living memory, winning two League Championships, the FA Cup and the European Cup Winners Cup.

This book contains many wonderful memories of Everton, but the story it does not tell is how much easier my job as manager was during the time that Kevin Ratcliffe was my Captain.

Howard Kendall

Relaxing at home

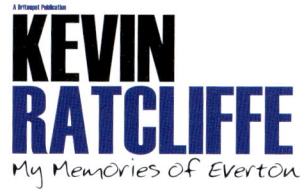

KEVIN RATCLIFFE
My Memories Of Everton

Kevin Ratcliffe My Memories of Everton
A Britespot Publication

First Published in Great Britain by
Britespot Publishing Solutions Limited
Chester Road, Cradley Heath, West Midlands B64 6AB

© Britespot October 2003

All rights reserved
No part of this publication may be reproduced, stored in a retrieval system, or transmitted, in any form or by any means (including photocopying) without the prior permission in writing of the author or the publisher, nor be otherwise circulated in any form of binding or cover other than that in which it is published and without a similar condition including this condition being imposed on the subsequent purchaser. Every effort has been made to ensure the accuracy of any material within this publication. However, the publisher will not accept any responsibility for accuracy of content or the opinions expressed by the author.

ISBN 1 904103 25 1

Cover design and layout
© Britespot Publishing Solutions Limited

Kevin Ratcliffe Acknowledgments:
I would like to thank all the following people in no particular order:

My wife Sharon, who has always been there for me through the highs and lows of my career, my children, Caroline, Dean and Beth.

My Mum Hannah and Dad Bryan for providing the help and encouragement to get my career started as a professional footballer. Brothers Paul, Neville and Colin, plus Uncle Graham for all of the support both home and away and my sister Helen.

Sharon's mother and father, Jean and Bob, for always being there for Sharon during all of the times I spent away with Everton and Wales. My Nan, Elsie, who sadly did not see me play at a senior level but who did buy me my first ever pair of football boots.

Colin Harvey, whose tremendous drive and enthusiasm formed the basis of my success and without whom I would not have become an Everton player. Howard Kendall for everything he did for Everton Football Club and for me personally.

Finally my thanks to everyone at Everton especially the staff at Bellefield Training Ground from the groundsman to the dinner ladies, all of whom made every day of training a real pleasure.

From Britespot Publishing: Roger Marshall, Paul Burns, Darren Cartwright, Chris Sweet, Chris Russell and Linda Perkins.

Publisher Acknowledgments:
The publisher would like to thank Kevin Ratcliffe, Jim Cadman for the inception of the 'My Memories' series, Simon 'Shakey' Shakeshaft, Tom Roe, Brendan Connelly, Ian Nannestad and Mark Platt.
Jen Little of Empics and Andy Cowie of Colorsport. Ceri Stennett of FAW, Jonathon Gammond of Welsh Football Collection, Wrexham County Borough Museum.

Finally Iain McCartney who, without his contribution, this book would not have been possible.

Photos © Empics, Colorsport, Action Images, Sporting Pictures and FAW Photo Archive.

Please Note. We have endeavoured to obtain copyright permission for usage of all the images contained within this publication, however, several images used in this publication are from Kevin Ratcliffe's personal collection, from old scrap books, albums, programmes etc... and we have been unable to establish clear copyright. The publishers would be pleased to hear from anyone who's copyright has been unintentionally infringed to avoid any further misuse in subsequent publications.

My FA Cup Final shirt & Souvenir Programme

CONTENTS
Chapters

Page

Me aged 10 months

Chapter 1

EARLY YEARS
From playing fields to Goodison Park

As a football-mad primary schoolboy, kicking a ball around playing fields, parks, back gardens or wherever, I never for one minute thought that some 16 years later I would have become Everton's most successful captain to date. As an Everton supporter back then, it was beyond even my wildest dreams.

Although I used to dream that I would play for them both at night, whilst tucked up in bed and when I was kicking a ball around with my mates that I would play for them, it was something that I never actually thought would happen in real life.

But not only did I achieve my boyhood ambition of signing for Everton, I went on to lead my beloved Toffees to the Football League Championship, FA Cup, FA Charity Shield and the European Cup Winner's Cup.

My dreams of becoming a professional footballer, like those of hundreds of other young boys, were, as I have said, always there. As I progressed from Deeside Primary as a nine or ten year old to the Flintshire Schoolboys under 13 and under 15 sides, those ambitions became stronger. By now, I was playing for Connah's Quay High School and I captained the side to the Clwyd Schools Football Association under 15 championships.

"There were of course others who wore the blue of Everton, whom I admired during my days on the terracing"

The next step on the ladder took me into the Welsh under 15 schools side and I won my first cap against Scotland at Ninian Park, a match that ended in a 2-2 draw. My second cap was perhaps more memorable, as it was against England at Wembley, but it also saw us lose 4-1. It was great to play there. The drive up to the stadium, walking up that tunnel, where hundreds of famous feet had walked before me. Little did I know at that time that I would be back again more than once in the years ahead.

Losing 4-1 was a big disappointment, but three of our players, including the goalkeeper, received injuries, although to be honest, we were clearly outplayed even when we were at full strength. Thankfully I can remember very little about that game, or the other schoolboy international that I played there. In fact the only memories that I do have are of Wayne Clarke, who was later to become an Everton team mate, playing for England and that the dressing rooms were very disappointing, as I expected something a bit grander.

My selection for the Welsh Schoolboy international side though provided me with a chance to step up onto the big stage.

I suppose, looking back, if Everton had not come for me I would have become a professional footballer with one of those other clubs, or perhaps with one nearer to home, as Chester and Wrexham had both been hovering in the shadows. I would certainly have gone to either of the latter two if they had promised me a chance of making the grade at senior level and possibly because of their locality I might have chosen them before the Londoners.

Chester would have been my preference, as I had been training with them off and on as a 14 year old and their manager Ken Roberts was someone that I liked and would have been quite happy to learn from. They had offered me schoolboy terms, but at that time I was walking around with my fingers crossed in the hope that Everton would make a move.

Aged 9 with my younger sister Helen

Unknown to me, the Toffees North Wales scout, George Ryan had been keeping a close eye on my progress and before I knew it, I had received an invitation to train at Bellefield. George had known of the Ratcliffe family's blue inclinations, but was quite persistent in his attempts to secure my signature. After countless visits and numerous telephone calls, he was invited to our house by my father and after agreeing to one or two minor points, I signed on the dotted line.

It wasn't as if Everton were any old club. They were MY club, a club with a great history and here I was, following in the footsteps of countless big name players, who had made their marks in the Football League in years gone by.

When I wasn't playing, I was always eager to get to Goodison Park and watch my blue shirted heroes. It was something special to be on the terraces during the late sixties and early seventies watching your favourite club. Everton had an exciting team in those days and included numerous players who could have walked into any other side in the First Division, whilst many of the opposition had at least one individual worth paying the admission money to watch.

My father Bryan was a staunch Evertonian, as were his three brothers. He was also a reasonable footballer himself playing for Everton as a teenager in the A and B teams.

I was only eight years old when I was taken to Goodison Park to watch Everton and in later years, it was a real family affair, with my father, his three brothers and my brother Paul. My father would slip the gateman half a crown (just over 12p in today's money) and we would watch the game from the back of the old stand.

My watching soon became limited, as I began to play more and more, but any opportunity that I had to get to Goodison, was taken.

So then, who were my favourite players, the ones that I hero-worshipped from the Gwladys Street End? Those whom I would go home and try and model myself on, practising their twists and turns, ball control and skill. The players whom I was determined to emulate in the years ahead.

My choice, would probably be the same as countless others who watched Everton during that particular time. There was no choice really, Colin Harvey, Howard Kendall and Alan Ball: 'The Holy Trinity'.

Colin Harvey, who began as an inside forward, went on to make the Everton number six shirt his own for almost six years. He was a local lad, who broke into the side as an 18 year old in 1963 for what was to be no ordinary debut (and one that would have frightened the life out of me), against AC Milan in the San Siro Stadium for a European Cup tie.

Like a good wine, Colin matured over the years but his sterling, whole hearted performances in the blue of Everton was not enough to win him regular recognition in the white of England. To me, it was a complete injustice that he only ever received one cap. When you think of the number of players and quite often the quality of players who play for England today, it makes you wonder why Colin did not win more caps to fill his trophy cabinet.

Imagine, one solitary cap against Malta in 1971 and that was it? Although thankfully, he had a League championship medal from 1970 and an FA Cup winners medal from 1966 to place alongside it, just rewards for his endeavours.

I would often watch in awe, as Colin strutted his stuff. Although not the tallest of players, he more than made up for his lack of inches with raw passion. His work rate, ball control and overall positional play made him the ideal half back or midfield player as the position became known.

Playing for Deeside Primary School, aged 10 (back row, far right)

Never a noted goalscorer, any that he did score whilst I was standing on the terracing made the afternoon all the more enjoyable. Of his 24 goals, one does stand out above the rest. Scored on Saturday April 23rd 1966, it was the only goal of the match against Manchester United, at Bolton's Burnden Park and it took Everton to Wembley for the FA Cup Final.

Sadly, all good things must come to an end and in 1974, after 380 appearances, he was transferred to Sheffield Wednesday. Devastated is the only word to describe my feelings.

The second of the three was Howard Kendall, a player whose career should, like that of Colin Harvey's, yielded much more in the way of personal honours. Howard first came to my attention when I watched the 1964 FA Cup final between West Ham United and Preston North End. A match that saw him enter the record books as the youngest player, to appear in the prestigious match, just 20 days short of his 18th birthday. Adding my support to the Lancashire side (only for the afternoon), I was disappointed that a runners-up medal was his early birthday present.

In March 1967, Howard moved to Goodison in an £80,000 deal, stepping into the first team to play immediately behind Colin Harvey at left half, but when the following season got under way, he had switched to right half, the position that he was to make his own.

"It was the defenders that I kept a particularly close eye on when watching Everton or any other club for that matter"

His performances helped Everton to materialise into a Championship winning side, showing an improvement in their League form over the first three years of his Goodison Park career, leading up to the title success in 1970.

Sadly, his performances, whilst appreciated by myself and the Everton supporters failed to please the England hierarchy and Howard became one of the best players to grace the domestic scene yet never win international recognition.

Over 250 games later, the Everton engine room required a bit of maintenance work and after playing only a handful of games during the season 1973-74, he left for Birmingham City as part of the deal which took Bob Latchford in the opposite direction.

Some eight years later, he made a token return to Goodison Park, playing four games during the 1981-82 season.

Strangely though both Colin and Howard were later to retrace their steps and return to Goodison in the capacity of managers.

Completing the 'Holy Trinity' was Alan Ball, unmistakable out on the park, with his ginger hair and his white boots. He also stood out due to his dynamic performances with Everton and England following his transfer from Blackpool for a £110,000 British record fee. Unlike the previous two individuals, if the likes of Alf Ramsey had left Alan out of the England set up then they would have been looking for new employment!

Totally involved in every game and a player who led by example. No game was ever lost until the final whistle if he was playing. To say I idolised 'Bally' would be a big understatement and I used to think if I could ever be half as good as him, then I would be happy.

*Playing for the Everton
Youth team at 17 years old*

If a survey was ever carried out in an effort to find out who Everton's greatest ever player was, then Alan Ball would be up there. At times he walked a tightrope of controversy and his style of play won him few friends among his opponents, but he was adored on the Goodison Park terraces.

He played a big part in Everton's title triumph of 1969-70 and it came as something of a surprise when Harry Catterick allowed Arsenal to take him south for what was another record fee - £220,000. He was later to move to Southampton and it was perhaps fitting that his last game at the top level was against Everton, where he enjoyed his best years.

There were of course others who wore the blue of Everton, whom I admired during my days on the terracing.

Big Gordon West in goal, another former Blackpool player, who went on to cement his name into the history of Everton, playing over 300 games in a 12 year career. He had his critics, especially when he turned down the chance to travel with England to the 1970 World Cup in Mexico, choosing to stay with his family, but I rated him highly.

Defensive players perhaps caught my eye more than forwards, with Brian Labone and full back Tommy Wright being two more of the players whom I watched and eventually followed to Goodison.

Brian was a big no nonsense defender, but he played the game fairly and had something of an exemplary record for a player in that position, being booked only once in a career which spanned over 13 years. His 530 appearances are only a dozen short of Ted Sagar's record. It is worth noting, however, that the goalkeeper's career spanned nine more years. Brian is of course another player who would be up there amongst the Everton all time greats.

Our careers actually ran on something of a parallel, with Brian having watched Everton from the terraces as a youngster before going on to captain them to both League and FA Cup success. He also enjoyed a successful international career, playing 26 times for England.

Unfortunately, his playing days, which spanned some 13 years, came to a premature end due to an achilles tendon injury in a reserve-team fixture in September 1971.

Full back Tommy Wright, like myself, was as Evertonian through and through, but Tommy had the advantage of being a local lad, which gained him that extra respect from the man on the terrace. Although not one of the names that is immediately remembered as one of the Goodison Greats, there is no doubting the part played by Tommy in the quest for honours during his time at the club.

He took over one of the full back positions from another Everton legend, Alex Parker, in 1964 and went on to enjoy a lengthy career, which brought him 370 first team appearances as well as international honours. He was important member of that Everton side of the mid-sixties/early seventies, and his retirement left a big void in their defence.

As I said earlier, it was the defenders that I kept a particularly close eye on when watching Everton or any other club for that matter. But, I also paid quite a bit of attention to the forwards, as it enabled me to understand how they played, how they reacted to various situations like close marking or whatever and how they all had different strengths to their game which they used to try and get the better of their opposite number.

There was one forward in particular that I could not fail to admire and someone I still have much admiration for. His name was Joe Royle, a virtual goal machine, still considered Everton's best post war front man.

(left - right) Mom & Dad,
myself and wife Sharon

Joe was at one point the youngest player to pull on an Everton jersey in a Football League match, (that was of course until a certain Wayne Rooney came along!), making his debut at the age of 16 when he appeared against Blackpool at Bloomfield Road on January 15th 1965.

After only a handful of appearances during seasons 1965-66 and 1966-67, he began the following campaign in the number nine jersey and never looked back, scoring 119 goals in just over 270 appearances.

He used his physical attributes to the best advantages, becoming a key member of the side and winning a Championship medal in 1970 plus a handful of England caps, before losing his first team place early in season 1974-75 and moving to Manchester City. Later he was to move into management with varied success, but I am still convinced that he will make a bigger name for himself at this level in the future.

Joe, however, is pipped as Everton's greatest goalscorer by a man, whose mere mention immediately conjures up everything Everton – William Ralph Dean. Known to one and all as 'Dixie'.

"My selection for the Welsh Schoolboy international side though provided me with a chance to step up onto the big stage"

Not only was he Everton's best, he was arguably the best-ever in his position. A total of 399 League games produced 349 goals, while a further 32 FA Cup appearances saw various goalkeepers beaten 28 times. When digesting those statistics, one has to remember that the players of the twenties and thirties had to endure playing surfaces which were not as ideal as those of today's, while the playing kit and of course the match ball itself were much heavier. The modern day players are debatably in better physical condition, but I don't think any could surpass the likes of Dixie Dean, especially his 60 League goals during one season, 1927-28.

On the ground, or particularly in the air, Dixie terrorised defences up and down the country, but he must have been a joy to watch. I would certainly have loved to have witnessed his goalscoring performances in the flesh, but thankfully I did not have to face anyone like him during my own playing days.

Many players today add to their pensions or whatever by doing after-dinner speaking. Give a brief account of their career, tell a few funny tales, get a bite to eat, a few drinks and a four-figure fee. This, however, is nothing new, as Dixie Dean was perhaps the player who conceived this idea, as he used to hold audiences spellbound by his tales of goals and glory with Everton.

Dixie Dean is an integral part of Everton's long and chequered history, a history that began not too far from the current Goodison Park ground in 1878.

Goodison Park, a welcome sight to every Evertonian

Chapter 2

HISTORY
The Begining Of Everton Football Club

Like many other football teams, Everton Football Club had its origins in the church, with the young men of the time alternating between cricket in the summer and football in the winter. It wasn't, however, a case of what came first, the chicken or the egg scenario, as the St Domingo's Church Cricket Club was already a familiar local organisation before the football branch materialised in 1878.

Stanley Park, was even in those distant days, home to the club and a year after deciding to form a football team, the office bearers took the steps to become non-denominational, in an effort to attract better players. This followed a meeting in the Queens Head Hotel, close to the Ancient Everton Toffee House.

A new name was also decided upon and Everton Football Club was born.

Six years on after the club's first game at their Stanley Park ground on December 23rd 1879 against St Peter's, which resulted in a confidence boosting 6-0 win, professionalism was introduced.

> "If the sixties belonged to my heroes, then the seventies
> and eighties were my years at the club, contributing to
> the ongoing history of Everton Football Club"

Initial fixtures were mainly local, with details of the club's progress passing unnoticed outside the boundary of the city and its environs. Progress, however, was steady and the quality of players slowly improving, as did the standard of opposition. So much so in fact, that with the formation of the Football League, Everton were invited to become founder members along with another 11 clubs from the north and midlands.

Looking back on those bygone days, they must have been exciting times for the players of yesteryear, stepping up from playing local football and sometimes hastily arranged games, to organised fixtures, under official rules and against teams that they were totally unfamiliar with.

Within three years, the club was celebrating its first League Championship success, a far cry from their first trophy – the Liverpool Cup, won in 1883-84. The positive steps forward, culminating with that initial title triumph in 1891 were also to bring frustration, despair and in the end a new dawn.

The club's Anfield headquarters were the Sandon Hotel and landlord John Houlding, a typical businessman, felt that as the club was slowly becoming more popular and of course successful, they should be paying more rent. Houlding also enjoyed the sole right to sell refreshments at the ground.

Without having much of a choice, the club reluctantly paid Houlding's demands, but in January 1892, after numerous squabbles amongst the committee, the St Domingo's organist, a leading accountant, announced that he had found a new location which could be developed into the club headquarters. Not everyone was for the change, but in the end, they felt that it would probably be for the best. Soon after moving to the opposite side of Stanley Park, the club formed itself into a limited company and never looked back.

The FA Cup was won for the first time in 1906 and a second championship followed in 1915, but the Great War soon put paid to any hopes of more success.

Everton legend Dixie Dean

Dixie Dean's 60 League goals in season 1927-28 brought the First Division title back to Goodison Park, but having enjoyed continuous First Division status since the League's formation, it came as a severe blow when the club was dragged into Division Two following a disastrous season two years later.

Being relegated, however, gave the club something of a jolt and not only did they immediately jump back into the top flight as champions, they lifted the First Division title once again, the season after that, 1931-32.

Once more the hopes of continued success floundered with only the FA Cup in 1933 finding a space in the Everton boardroom.

Five League titles and two F. A. Cup successes unfortunately do not take up much space on the honours board during the pre-war period, but alongside the name of Dixie Dean, there were many other notable individuals who pulled on the famous blue shirt, in whose steps I was proud to follow.

Individuals such as Walter Balmer, a stocky full back who made 290-odd appearances between 1897 and 1907. Cliff Britton, a notable half back of some considerable skill who went onto win England honours, alongside Joe Mercer and Stan Cullis. Mercer himself made over 180 appearances for Everton in the 1930s and the first season after the Second World War.

Alec Troup, the supplier of many of Dixie Dean's goals, was a diminutive, ball playing winger in the old mould and a Scottish international, who played almost 260 games for Everton, while the likes of Jimmy Stein, Jock Thomson, Alex Young (mark one), Billy Cook, Richard Boyle and John Macconnachie were others from north of the border to etch their names into Evertonian folklore.

Others like Tom Booth, Edgar Chadwick, Tom Fleetwood, Fred Geary, Harold Hardman and John Bell, yet another Scot, all played their part in establishing the club during the earlier days of their history.

Moving into the post-war period , there are a host of memorable players and games that are much more familiar to me and I dare say the majority of the present-day Everton supporters. But again, sadly, the honours are few and far between and there was also a spell of three consecutive seasons in the Second Division, between 1951-52 and 1953-54.

Retaining our rightful place in the top flight saw a period of consolidation in the late 1950s before stepping closer to that coveted top spot. After 16 long seasons, the record books once again showed Everton as Football League Champions in 1962-63, with an FA Cup victory following in 1965-66.

I have already mentioned one or two of the players who graced the team in those halcyon days, but there were also others worth a mention. Names such as Roy Vernon, a fellow Welshman and a skilful inside forward with an eye for goal. Dave Hickson a centre forward who plied his trade on both sides of Stanley Park and the diminutive Bobby Collins, a Scottish inside forward of the old school.

Jimmy Gabriel, Alex Scott and the still-revered Alex Young, were a trio of Scotsmen who played a big part in the triumphs of 1963 and 1966. Gabriel was a £30,000 signing from Dundee in 1960 and proved to be worth every penny of that fee. A fine defensive wing half.

My footballing home, Goodison Park

Scott and Young on the other hand were forwards. The former a skilful winger who moved south from Glasgow Rangers, while the latter, 'The Golden Vision', a former Hearts player should perhaps have scored a few more goals than he did, but led the front line unselfishly and was hero-worshipped by the Goodison Park crowd for the wonderful memories that he provided.

"A new name was also decided upon and Everton Football Club was born"

The 1970 Championship saw the likes of Jimmy Husband, Keith Newton, Johnny Morrisey and John Hurst in the side, while the early seventies also produced players like Bob Latchford, a big bustling centre forward and Mick Lyons a no-nonsense defender.

Thankfully, we did not have to wait another 16 seasons for another championship, as Everton dominated the League again in season 1969-70, but it was not until the mid 1980s that the silver polish was again an item on the Everton shopping list, but we were then to buy it in bulk.

If the sixties belonged to my heroes, then the seventies and eighties were my years at the club, contributing to the ongoing history of Everton Football Club.

An Agreement

made the *24th* day of *JUNE* 19*77* between *JAMES GREENWOOD* of *GOODISON PARK LIVERPOOL* in the COUNTY OF *MERSEYSIDE* the Secretary of and acting pursuant to Resolution and Authority for and on behalf of the *EVERTON* FOOTBALL CLUB of *GOODISON PARK LIVERPOOL* (hereinafter referred to as the Club) of the one part and *KEVIN RATCLIFFE* of *61 COURTLAND DRIVE ASTON PARK QUEENSFERRY* in the COUNTY OF .... Apprentice Football Player (hereinafter referred to as the Player) of the other part Whereby it is agreed as follows :—

1. The Player hereby agrees to play in an efficient manner and to the best of his ability for the Club.

2. The Player shall attend the Club's ground or any other place decided upon by the Club for the purposes of or in connection with his training as a Player pursuant to the instructions of the Secretary, Manager, or Trainer of the Club, or of such other person, or persons as the Club may appoint.

3. The Player shall do everything necessary to get and keep himself in the best possible condition so as to render the most efficient service to the Club, and will carry out all the training and other instructions of the Club through its representative officials.

4. The Player shall observe and be subject to all the Rules, Regulations and Bye-Laws of The Football Association, and any other Association, League, or Combination of which the Club shall be a member. And this Agreement shall be subject to any action which shall be taken by The Football Association under their Rules for the suspension or termination of the Football Season, and if any such suspension or termination shall be decided upon the payment of wages shall likewise be suspended or terminated, as the case may be.

5. The Player shall not engage in any business or live in any place which the Directors (or Committee) of the Club may deem unsuitable, provided that the Club shall, at the request of the Player or his Parent or Guardian, allow the Player to continue his further education or take up suitable vocational training.

6. If the Player shall be guilty of serious misconduct or breach of the disciplinary Rules of the Club, the Club may, on giving 14 days' notice to the said Player, or the Club may, on giving 28 days' notice to the said Player, on any reasonable grounds, terminate this Agreement and dispense with the services of the Player in pursuance of the Rules of all such Associations, Leagues,

My first Everton Contract (front)

Chapter 3

MY EVERTON DAYS
Finally making the First Team

The seventies were almost at an end, as was my first contract with the club, and I was beginning to have a few nagging doubts as to whether or not they would renew it. Despite progressing through the junior ranks and playing regularly in the reserves, I seemed to be no nearer to making that important step up to the senior side. I was becoming desperate just to get my foot in the first-team door and despite my love for the club, perhaps if I wanted to make the grade as a professional footballer then it was going to be away from Liverpool L4 4EL.

Having given myself until the end of the 1979-80 season to achieve my goal, it came as something of a relief to be included in the squad for the UEFA Cup 1st round second leg tie against Feyenoord at home. Having lost the first leg 2-0, we were really up against it and I didn't really expect to make the starting line-up. In the end, I was named amongst the substitutes and the closest I got to the action was warming up from time to time along the touchline.

> "My debut did not make any big headlines in the following mornings newspapers, but any comments were, thankfully, complimentary"

One month later, I was back in the frame of things, travelling with the squad to Norwich. This time, however, I didn't even make the bench, losing out to Peter Eastoe.

I had actually roomed with Peter for our overnight stop in East Anglia and not only did he pip me for that place on the substitutes bench, but I ended up losing sleep and being out of pocket. He became a dad that night and following a few telephone calls, he woke me up to share in his good news and then asked if he could borrow £5 to send his dear wife some flowers!

You would have thought that the excitement of the early hours would have been too much for him or my generosity would have seen him quite happy to let me take the substitute's shirt, but no chance.

The 0-0 draw at Carrow Road on November 3rd, was the second goalless draw on the trot and this was followed by a 2-0 defeat at Middlesborough. Despite a 5-1 win in the next fixture against Leeds United at home, we were to win only two of the next 15 games. Things were certainly not looking good.

After losing 2-1 at home to Liverpool our next fixture was just as difficult, against second-placed Manchester United away.

Once again, I was included in the squad and we travelled along the East Lancs Road early in the day for the evening kick off, stopping at the Northenden Post House for a few hours rest and a bite to eat before continuing to Old Trafford.

Little did I know that John Gidman had taken ill and as I came down for our pre-match meal and team talk I thought that Mike Lyons was having me on when he pulled me to one side and told me that because of John's condition he thought that I had a very good chance of playing.

Thinking no more about what I considered a wind up, I enjoyed the meal. But, as I was leaving the dining room, manager Gordon Lee called me over and confirmed that Mike's little chat was no wind up and that I was indeed playing against United.

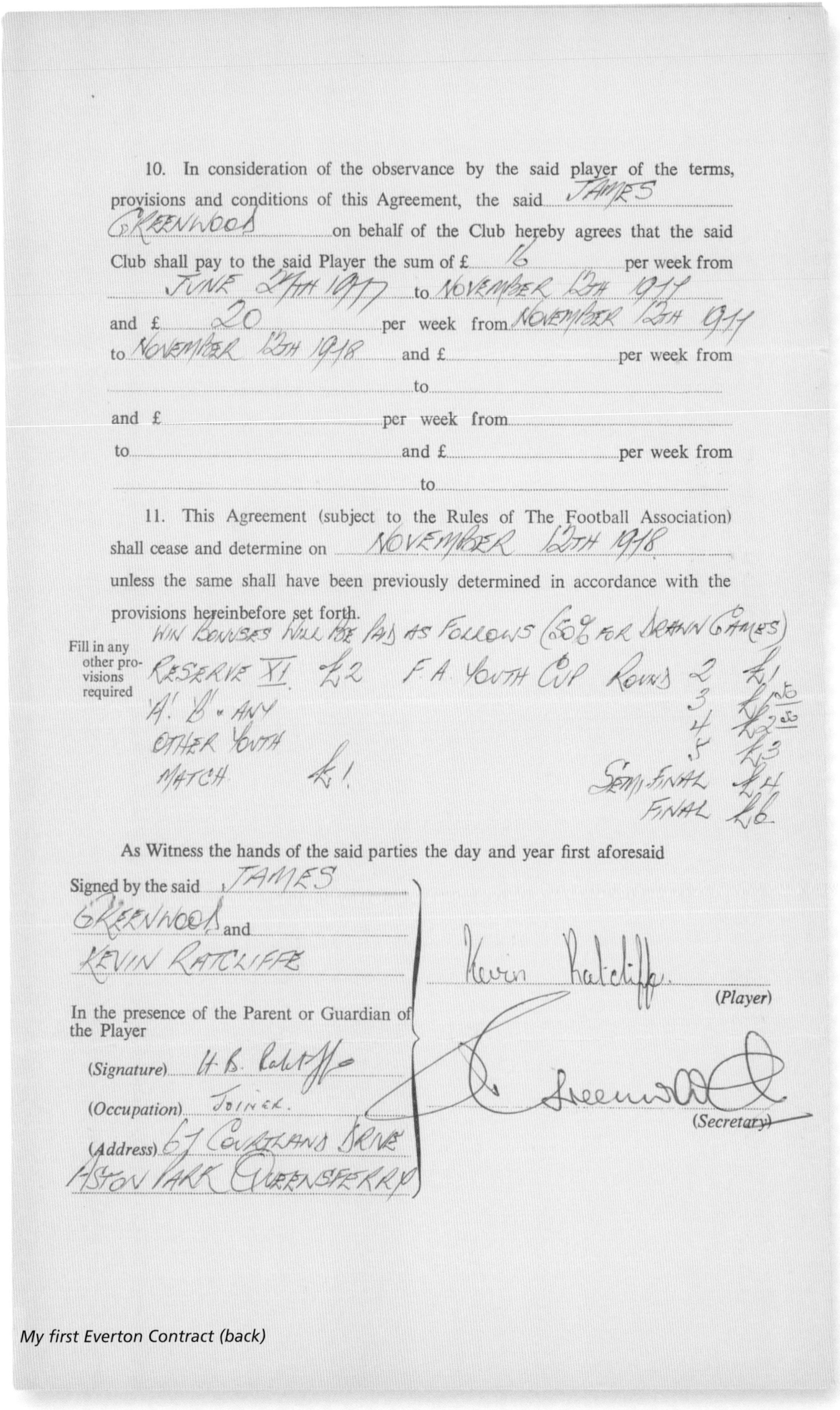

10. In consideration of the observance by the said player of the terms, provisions and conditions of this Agreement, the said _JAMES GREENWOOD_ on behalf of the Club hereby agrees that the said Club shall pay to the said Player the sum of £ _16_ per week from _JUNE 27TH 1977_ to _NOVEMBER 12TH 1977_ and £ _20_ per week from _NOVEMBER 12TH 1977_ to _NOVEMBER 12TH 1978_ and £ _____ per week from _____ to _____ and £ _____ per week from _____ to _____ and £ _____ per week from _____ to _____

11. This Agreement (subject to the Rules of The Football Association) shall cease and determine on _NOVEMBER 12TH 1978_ unless the same shall have been previously determined in accordance with the provisions hereinbefore set forth.

Fill in any other provisions required

WIN BONUSES WILL BE PAID AS FOLLOWS (50% FOR DRAWN GAMES)
RESERVE XI £2   F.A YOUTH CUP ROUND 2 £1
A. B. ANY   3 £1.50
OTHER YOUTH   4 £2.50
MATCH   £1   5 £3
                          SEMI FINAL £4
                          FINAL £6

As Witness the hands of the said parties the day and year first aforesaid

Signed by the said _JAMES GREENWOOD_ and _KEVIN RATCLIFFE_

Kevin Ratcliffe
(Player)

In the presence of the Parent or Guardian of the Player

(Signature) _H. B. Ratcliffe_

(Occupation) _JOINER._

(Address) _67 COURTLAND DRIVE ASTON PARK QUEENSFERRY_

Greenwood
(Secretary)

My first Everton Contract (back)

Thankfully, my family were within easy travelling distance of Manchester and a quick, rather incoherent, telephone call to my dad enabled him to get over in time for the kick off, along with my uncle Graham and brother Paul.

If I had been given a choice of venue in which to make my debut, I might have chosen a smaller ground, and against a smaller team, but they don't come much bigger and better than Old Trafford and Manchester United, do they? Goodison Park would have been perhaps the ideal choice, but it would probably have been more nerve wracking.

I didn't have too much time to be nervous, and looking back, I have to say that I enjoyed the occasion, especially as we managed to keep United at bay in a 0-0 draw. An early touch and a good through ball to Brian Kidd settled me down and I managed to fit into the team, playing as sweeper, as we came away with that precious point.

"Despite progressing through the junior ranks and playing regularly in the reserves, I seemed to be no nearer to making that important step up to the senior side"

My debut did not make any big headlines in the following mornings newspapers, but any comments were, thankfully, complimentary.

I had waited so long for my chance and I was glad that I had made the most of it. However, John Gidman quickly recovered, too quickly for my liking, and reclaimed his place, with Billy Wright, whose right half berth I had taken over, moving back to his own position.

Before the 1979-80 season came to an end though, I was back in the first team, playing against West Ham United in the FA Cup semi-final replay at Elland Road and in the League fixture, three days later, against Tottenham Hotspur. Both games, sadly, ending in defeat. The cup-tie was obviously the biggest disappointment, as I felt that we should have won. With the game slipping away, Bob Latchford gave us an equaliser, but Frank Lampard sneaked in to snatch a late winner.

After playing in two consecutive games, I was brought back down to earth with a massive bump, finding out that I had been dropped for the match against Southampton as I sat watching the Granada TV Friday night football programme 'Kick-Off'.

With only three fixtures remaining, I didn't hold out any hopes of playing in the first team again that season, but my brief flirtation with first-team football made me even more determined not just to make the grade as a professional footballer, but to establish myself in the Everton first team.

*Me and Mike Lyons out jump Liverpool's David Fairclough during the
Merseyside derby at Goodison Park in the FA Cup 4th Round on 24th July 1981*

Chapter 4

HUNGRY FOR SUCCESS

1980-81 Season

Most footballers look forward to, and certainly enjoy their summer break. But for me, the close season of 1980 was nothing more than a major inconvenience. I had made my Everton debut, played in a couple of other games and was desperate for more.

Pre-season took us to Spain and as well as topping up my tan, I must have done a few things right as I found myself in the starting line up for the opening game of the 1980-81 season against Sunderland at Roker Park. It was an unfamiliar position for me though, left back, but who cared, it was first-team football.

It was, however, not the best of starts, as we lost 3-1.

I managed to keep my place for the opening four League fixtures, one win, one draw and two defeats, before stepping back into the Central League team, losing my place to John Bailey, a bubbly, larger than life character, who became a good friend.

I then had to wait some time before making a return to the first team against Manchester City at Goodison on Boxing Day. Obviously, it was disappointing being out of the first team picture for so long, but the disappointment of being out of the side was eased considerably in November, when I was awarded my first senior Welsh cap.

"I had made my Everton debut, played in a couple of other games and was desperate for more"

This ultimate honour came against Czechoslovakia in a World Cup qualifier at Cardiff and even although I was only a replacement for the injured Joey Jones of Liverpool, it was still an unbelievable feeling.

My return to the Everton first team was an ideal, though slightly belated, Christmas present and it saw me back in my favoured, more familiar position in the centre of the defence. Although we lost 2-0 against Manchester City on Boxing Day and 1-0 at Middlesborough the following day, I kept my place for all but four of the remaining 20 League fixtures.

It was not all joy though, as a black cloud overshadowed our FA Cup 6th round tie against Manchester City at Goodison. So near to Wembley, with high hopes of going all the way, we were leading City 2-1 when I became involved in a stupid incident with Tommy Hutchison, due more to my own naivety.

The more experienced City player had been playing up to me for most of the match, backing into me, trampling on my toes and being quite honestly, something of a complete nuisance. I gradually became fed up with it all and with Hutchison shielding the ball down towards the corner flag, I completely lost it. Down he went and off I went!

Paul Power, later to become an Everton team mate, went on to score an equaliser for City and in the Maine Road replay we were completely outplayed, losing 3-1.

Thankfully that incident did not cost me my place in the team, but it did teach me a lesson.

I had returned to full back, playing on both flanks, but for the final three games of 1980-81 I wore the number four shirt, the one that was to become more or less my own in the years ahead.

Taking a throw-in against Stoke City at Goodison Park, 13th February 1982

Chapter 5

PLAYING FOR MY HERO
1981-82 Season

As the 1981-82 season got underway, with Howard Kendall, one of my boyhood heroes now at the helm, I found myself watching the opening fixture against Birmingham City from the stand. Despite the new manager having wanted to sign me when he was with Blackburn Rovers, I thought that he had now gone off me and that I was going to play Central League football until someone else's misfortune gave me a break.

Much to my surprise though, the name of Ratcliffe appeared on the first eleven's team sheet for the second match of the season against Leeds United. Once again it was at full back, but we only managed a 1-1 draw.

"Would I ever obtain a place in the line up on a regular basis?"

I kept my place for the next five games, but my form began to drop and with the crowd not being exactly enthusiastic towards me, my overall confidence slowly deteriorated. A couple of months in the reserves followed.

Results were varied in the opening half of the campaign and Howard Kendall ended up picking himself against Notts County towards the end of November. This fixture also saw me return to the fold, with the boss perhaps thinking that he could keep an eye on me and offer some encouragement, and after a run of three defeats, we managed a 2-2 draw.

It wasn't the start of a good run, as we lost the following game at Arsenal, but we finally seemed to have turned the corner, as we did not lose again for another eight games and I managed to keep my place in the line-up.

The manager left me out of the side in February for a month. Several exchanges of words and opinions seemed to have swung things in my favour with another run in the line-up, but I once again found myself omitted from the team and missed the final five games of the season.

Would I ever obtain a place in the line up on a regular basis? I was beginning to have my doubts. It was so frustrating. A run in the side then back into the reserves. I was in something of a dilemma.

Obviously I wanted to have more opportunities of first team-football on a regular basis, but I didn't want to leave Goodison to obtain this. However, if the current situation continued, then I would possibly have to sit down and consider my options very carefully.

After much thought and soul searching, biting my tongue, I told Howard Kendall that I wanted to leave the club. He listened to what I had to say and replied if that was what I wanted, then he would put me on the transfer list and see what developed.

*Rising above Man Utd's Norman Whitseide in the
FA Cup 6th Round tie at Old Trafford, 11th March 1983*

Chapter 6

AN UNCERTAIN TIME AHEAD
1982-83 Season

If my future was going to be away from Everton, then Howard Kendall had to build his team around other players and my appearances would be few and far between. As it was, I made only one League appearance, due to Mark Higgins being injured, between August and the end of October, although I managed to play in one of the League Cup ties against Newport County.

"The crowd began to become more appreciative and I began to enjoy life at Goodison Park once again"

Our aggregate victory against Newport saw us drawn against Arsenal, a much sterner test and as the fixtures worked out, we ended up playing them on November 9th, 13th and 23rd. The first and last were in the League Cup, when we drew 1-1 at home, the replay was a disaster though, as we lost 3-0.

A devastating 5-0 defeat at the hands Liverpool, made worse by it being at home, had got November off to a bad start and Howard Kendall decided that we had to do something to strengthen the defence. Into the side to face Arsenal in the League Cup came Jim Arnold in goal and at number two came Gary Stevens, with me at three. We were all to keep our places for the League match against Nottingham Forest, with Gary like me only missing one other League match that season. All thoughts of a move were now forgotten.

I missed the visit of Birmingham City to Goodison, but returned to the side the following Saturday at Ipswich. This time, however, I was handed the number four shirt and it was about to come more or less my personal property for the remainder of my Everton career.

It is surprising what a good run in the team can do for your confidence. A few cobwebs were blown away, my form improved, the crowd began to become more appreciative and I began to enjoy life at Goodison Park once again.

Not only that, I finally broke my scoring duck, snatching the only goal against Norwich City at Carrow Road on January 22nd. Even in my own modest words, it was a good goal. Honest! A worthy match winner.

Collecting the ball, I passed it out to Adrian Heath and moved forward for the return. Eventually, or perhaps reluctantly, he threaded the ball back through to me and taking it in my stride, I hit it high into the Norwich net from all of 18 yards.

So, 1982-83 was indeed a memorable season, with my first goal and my eventual breakthrough into becoming a first-team regular. Oddly enough, it could have turned out completely differently if Howard Kendall had revealed to me that both Ipswich Town and Stoke City had made enquiries about me, I could have found myself at another club, yearning for the familiar Gwladys Street.

*My FA Cup Winner's Medal and
Souvenir Programme from 1984*

Chapter 7

FA CUP GLORY
1983-84 Season

At long last, I felt that I had arrived as a professional footballer, but there were still a few black clouds on the not too distant horizon.

Refreshed from my summer break and raring to get the new League campaign off to a satisfactory start, my plans were somewhat put on hold and my competitive season did not get underway until the beginning of September, because I was forced to miss the first two fixtures due to suspension. I wasn't too clever in a pre-season friendly against Walsall, receiving my marching orders after an act of retaliation on a home team player who had enjoyed kicking Kevin Richardson around the pitch for the best part of the match. The referee felt that I had crossed the dividing line and felt that I should cool my heels in the dressing room.

"We would have turned up in jeans and t-shirts if it meant that we would be FA Cup winners"

To say that season 1983-84 got off to an indifferent start is something of an understatement with six wins, six draws and nine defeats up until Christmas. The only real bright spot was my first match as captain of Everton Football Club, against Arsenal at Highbury on November 19th, due to an injury to Mark Higgins. This again highlighted just how things can quickly change in the game of football.

Surprisingly enough, the turn of the year brought a change in fortune, with League Cup and FA Cup ties, bringing a welcome relief from the weekly grind of the Football League.

The League Cup had begun back in October at Chesterfield and a victory over two legs, was followed by further progress against Coventry City and West Ham United. By the end of January, we had played a further five cup-ties, as well as three League fixtures, and had made it through to the semi-final of the competition, but had not progressed beyond the fourth round of the more respected FA Cup. Gillingham were the stumbling block here, holding us to two 0-0 draws.

By the end of February we had finally managed to dispose of them, as well as Shrewsbury Town and were looking forward to a Wembley date in the League Cup final against none other than Liverpool. A 0-0 draw failed to set Wembley alight, while the replay at Maine Road, with its solitary winning goal for the Anfield side brought thorough disappointment to everyone associated with the club.

At the same time, it did, however, make us even more determined to reach the FA Cup final and make the return to the north London venue. Notts County were to put up a gallant fight in the quarter-finals, while Southampton could perhaps have considered themselves to be unlucky to lose the Highbury semi-final 1-0. At the end of the day though, we managed to obtain a result that was satisfactory to ourselves.

Another new suit to be measured up for, so we could look our best on the big day, but we would have turned up in jeans and t-shirts if it meant that we would be FA Cup winners at the end of the afternoon.

This time, with no disrespect to our opponent's Watford, we were very confident of lifting the silverware. As it was, they put up little in the way of resistance and goals from Andy Gray and Graeme Sharpe saw the name of Everton inscribed on the famous old trophy for the first time since 1966.

If I was up in the clouds following that May afternoon, then I was like an astronaut orbiting the earth at the end of the following season, 1984-85. We had always lived in the shadows of Harry Catterick's majestical sides, but in the months ahead, new names were going to be etched into the history of Everton Football Club.

My winner's medal and Souvenir programme from the European Cup Winner's Cup Final

Chapter 8

EUROPEAN SUCCESS AT LAST
1984-85 Season

The season that was to bring so much, got off to an ideal start, with a Charity Shield victory at Wembley against those troublesome red shirts from over the park. It was only an own goal, but any success over that lot is well worth celebrating.

Our League campaign, however, began with two defeats, against Tottenham and West Bromwich, which gave us something of a shake, but it was the end of November before we had suffered another two. We went top of the First Division after beating Leicester City 3-0 at the beginning of November, a week after a scintillating 5-0 display against Manchester United at home. A match that is still fondly talked about today.

We slipped a little in the following weeks, before returning to the top on January 12th where we remained for the rest of the campaign. A 28 match unbeaten run ended at Nottingham Forest on May 11th, but this hiccup mattered little, as we had secured the Championship three days earlier against West Ham United, with a 3-0 home victory. My defensive partner Derek Mountfield scoring an unlikely double.

"My proudest moment as a player? You bet"

As in the previous season, things were hotting up in the cup competitions. The League Cup had, perhaps thankfully, been discarded by the wayside following an instantly forgettable home defeat against Grimsby Town. In the others, we were on course to retain the FA Cup and more importantly, we had made steady progress in the European Cup Winner's Cup.

We reached the final of the Cup Winners Cup following one of the most memorable nights that Goodison Park had seen, with the 3-1 defeat of Bayern Munich. While Luton Town were beaten 2-1 in the FA Cup semi-final, producing two major cup finals in the space of three days in May.

Crossing the English Channel to Rotterdam was first on the itinerary, where we faced Rapid Vienna and on a truly memorable night, we climbed a pinnacle that had always eluded the club and lifted the European Cup Winner's Cup.

Manager Howard Kendall had done his homework in the days and weeks leading up to the game and as we ran out for the biggest game in our careers, we knew what to expect and what we had to do if we wanted to claim victory. Thankfully, everything went to plan and we won 3-1. My proudest moment as a player? You bet.

Before making a triumphant return to Liverpool, where for once, the city would be decked in blue rather than red, we, like many of our supporters, had to stop off in London due to a little matter of the FA Cup final.

Opponents Manchester United, held no fears as we had already beaten them twice that season, once in the League Cup and, as previously in that devastating 5-0 performance in the League.

Despite being confident, we were also tired, as the game ground into extra time. United had Kevin Moran sent off for a reckless challenge on Peter Reid. But following that set back, they suddenly came to life and a Norman Whiteside goal was enough to give them the cup and make sure that we did not have to have an extension built on to the trophy cabinet back at Goodison Park.

We sensed that we could be on the verge of something big as a team, but you can never take anything for granted, especially in football.

A race for the ball with Ian Rush during the FA Cup Final

Chapter 9

A SEASON TO FORGET

1985-86 Season

As it turned out, we never got to take our place in the European Cup and compete against the elite, as events in the Hysel Stadium a matter of days after our Rotterdam triumph saw all English sides banned from playing in European football.

> "The only real bright spot to look back
> on was my goal against Liverpool at Anfield"

Our defence of the League Championship stuttered at the end, despite scoring nine goals in the final two fixtures. A draw at Nottingham Forest and a 1-0 defeat at Oxford proving very costly indeed. Second place was the best we could manage.

It wasn't that we had played badly throughout the winter, we had two five-game runs without losing a goal and our record was comparable to that of the previous season. It was just those two away fixtures when it mattered most that had let us down.

They say bad luck comes in threes and in 1986, I would have certainly agreed with anyone who contributed to that theory. No European appearances, losing out to Liverpool in the League and our third FA Cup Final appearance in succession bringing additional disappointment, with Liverpool clinching the double following a 3-1 win. An ankle injury also kept me out of action for three weeks.

The only real bright spot to look back on was my goal against Liverpool at Anfield in February in our 2-0 win.

With the League Championship Trophy, 9th May 1987

Chapter 10

CHAMPIONS AGAIN
1986-87 Season

Determination is a great thing and can help you achieve numerable goals. Following our disappointments in May 1986, it carried us forward again in the following season.

"The disappointments of the previous season were still fresh in all our minds"

We began where we left off, Wembley, with a repeat performance of the FA Cup final. Liverpool this time were rather subdued and the Charity Shield was shared following a 1-1 draw.

The disappointments of the previous season were still fresh in all our minds despite the summer break and we were even more determined than usual to regain some of the 1985 trophy success.

It was eight games before we lost our unbeaten record and then we lost two in a row to the North London pairing of Tottenham Hotspur and Arsenal. However, by the end of the year, we were back on track with 22 goals for and only two against between December 20th and January 1st keeping us well on course in our quest for reclaiming the title.

Both domestic cup competitions proved fruitless, an unusual occurrence for us, with Wimbledon ending our FA Cup hopes with a 3-1 defeat and Liverpool beating us 1-0 in the League Cup. The League though, was beginning to take on a very different picture.

By April, we were sitting in a promising position, as Liverpool, forever the yardstick, began to stutter. However, failing to get a victory, or even a point, in our confrontation at the end of that month caused a few missed beats of the heart as well as a massive disappointment. Mainly because this would more or less have guaranteed us the title, as we were six points clear at that time. We now just had to keep plodding away.

A point against Manchester City at home was also viewed as rather unsatisfactory, with only three fixtures remaining and the need to conclude matters as soon as possible rather than having the outcome of the Championship drag on until the final day of the season.

Thankfully, it did not come to such a scenario, with Pat Van den Hauwe's goal at Norwich on May 4th, two days after the City game, giving us not only two points, but also the Championship itself for the second time in three years. The journey from East Anglia back to Merseyside, for once, did not seem so long.

A pre-season photocall

Chapter 11

INJURY NIGHTMARE
1987-88 Season

Over the past four seasons, I had more or less been an ever present, missing only nine League games during that period. However, the 1987-88 season was to be one of much disappointment, as it came to a premature end on January 9th during a third round FA Cup tie against Sheffield Wednesday at Hillsborough.

With only a few minutes still to play before the interval, I attempted to cut out a through ball from a Wednesday player and felt a twinge in my groin and that was that.

Six to eight weeks I was told that I would miss, but I thought that I was going to prove the doctors wrong by making an earlier return. Training was resumed within five weeks. I was beginning to feel good within myself, when I had a recurrence of the injury, forcing me back into the hands of the doctors and extending my spell on the sidelines.

"I attempted to cut out a through ball and felt a twinge in my groin and that was that"

Arsenal beat us in the semi-final of the League, while Liverpool ended our FA Cup hopes in the fifth round, with a 1-0 defeat. We had now faced Liverpool in cup competition in four out of the past five seasons. In the League though, it was so frustrating being unable to contribute anything, as the rest of the lads fought it out at the top.

We only lost two games between March 9th and May 7th, but the title had been lost and the best we could manage was fourth place. It was certainly a case of 'if only I had not got injured' as I am sure that I would have made a difference.

These things happen though and there is nothing at all that you can do about it.

A tough tackle on Liverpool's Ian Rush during the FA Cup Final

Chapter 12

NEIGHBOURS FROM HELL
1988-89 Season

It was October 8th before I returned to first-team action, against Southampton at Goodison and fortunately for me, at least, I only missed a couple of other fixtures during the season.

"Perhaps we were unfortunate that Liverpool were still ruling the roost"

A season that saw us finish in eighth position, our lowest for seven years.

Wembley, on the other hand was becoming something of a second home, as a good FA Cup run, after something of a shaky couple of early rounds, saw us reach the final. Perhaps we were unfortunate that Liverpool were still ruling the roost and they took the trophy to Anfield by the odd goal in five.

Against Crystal Palace, 7th April 1991

Chapter 13

INTO THE NINETIES
1989-90 to 1991-1992 Seasons

Having slipped to eighth in the First Division at the end of 1988-89, we managed to climb back up a couple of places the following year. Unknown to everyone though, Everton Football Club were destined to become a mid-table club for the foreseeable future.

During season 1989-90, I only managed two dozen appearances and was missing from the line up between October and December and again between the end of March and the final league fixture of the season.

> ## "I was now the old man of the team, with only Graeme Sharp still playing from the squad that was around when I made my debut"

I failed to make the starting line-up for the first couple of games of 1990-91, with Martin Keown, who had taken my place the previous season taking over. Having been a first team player for the best part of ten years, I was now almost 30 years old, there was always the threat of a promising youngster coming through and threatening the old legs.

Age mattered nothing, as I still felt that I had something to offer the team and I did maintain a certain level of fitness. Once I got back into the side for the third game of 1990-91, after making an appearance as substitute in the second, I was difficult to dislodge, missing only one other fixture. There was life in the old dog yet.

I was now the old man of the team, with only Graeme Sharp still playing from the squad that was around when I made my debut. We had some good players at that time, despite not exactly setting the hills on fire.

Season 1991-92 was to see the end of the dream, as I lost my place in early September, with John Ebbrell claiming my coveted number four jersey. I managed a couple of League appearances at left back in October and another in the League Cup at Watford.

On December 4th, against Leeds United at Goodison Park, also in the League Cup, I once again pulled on the number four shirt, but unknown to me at the time, this was to be my last appearance for the Toffees. It was certainly not the way I would have wanted to bow out, a 4-1 defeat in front of a meagre 25 odd thousand, but I could not go on for ever.

The arrival of 1991 heralded my departure from Everton, going onto the transfer list for a short period before joining Dundee on loan and then departing for Cardiff City.

Leaving Everton was certainly a wrench, the worst day of my life to be more exact. But, I had my medals, my memories and most of all no matter what my future held I had played for Everton, my team.

Chapter 14

GREAT PLAYERS OF MY ERA
From Everton

Neville Southall

Best in the world. A really good friend on and off the park and still is. Before he could drive, we shared lifts down to the Wales games. Between us, we had an excellent understanding.

Gary Stevens

If he wasn't a footballer, he would have been an athlete. So much energy on the pitch.

Dave Watson

Typical old-fashioned centre half. Great at his job and one of the best headers of a ball I have seen. Another player that I had a good understanding with.

Mark Higgins

A very unlucky player. He could easily have been one of the best, if it had not been for injuries. One of the most complete and bravest players that I have played with.

John Bailey

Great character and very funny. Not many wingers gave him the run around.

Pat Van den Hauwe

Good defender who kept everything simple. It was also very rare for him to give the ball away.

Derek Mountfield

Exceptional goalscorer for a centre half and a major threat at set pieces. Not the classiest of players, but he knew his limitations.

Trevor Steven

One of the best I have played with. Excellent all-round player. Although he was very quiet off the pitch, he could also be very witty.

Paul Bracewell

Another quiet lad. Very fit and someone who did the job required of him very well. Had an excellent understanding with Peter Reid.

Kevin Sheedy

A good friend whose company I enjoyed. We changed next to each other and shared a room on away trips. The best left foot I have ever seen. He created so much for the team.

Kevin Richardson

A player who could fit into any position in midfield due to his great versatility. I was very surprised to see him leave Goodison.

Alan Harper

Mr Versatile. He played everywhere for the team during his six years there. More than often, he was the first choice as substitute.

Adrian Heath

"Inchy" never really knew his best position. A bundle of energy who would score as many goals from midfield as he would from upfront.

Andy Gray

A larger than life character. Brought confidence to the team and did an excellent job for the club. A strong powerful individual player.

Graeme Sharp

Best target man I have played with. In my eyes the best in the world for three or four years.

Gary Lineker

Scored 40 goals in one season. Very quiet but kick-started his international career while at Goodison. Very strong on his feet in the box and never fell over. Scored many goals with simple tap-ins. He was the master poacher.

Peter Reid

He kept everything very simple, doing the right things. A bundle of energy, who never liked losing. Protected the back four. A brilliant individual to have in the dressing room. He certainly made my job a whole lot easier, as he was a great leader on the pitch.

Paul Power

Virtually an ever present in the Championship winning side of 1986-87. A seasoned professional who knew what it was all about. Great lad, who did an excellent job for us.

Bobby Mimms

Had the hard task of replacing big Nev, and although it was difficult for any of the second choice 'keepers to get ahead of the Welshman, he was most successful at covering for him. A big, strong, young goalkeeper, who impressed me a lot.

Alan Irvine

A fierce Scot who on his day was as good a winger as I have ever played with.

Two former Manchester United players, Norman Whiteside and Brian Kidd were others whom I played alongside at Everton, and are worth a mention.

Norman Whiteside

He was unfortunately moving towards the end of his career, with injuries taking their toll. He was, however, a tremendous player, who possessed incredible vision and touch. Had it not been for his injury problems, especially with United, I am convinced that he would have been one of the greatest players that Britain has produced.

Brian Kidd

Brian was another talented individual who Everton never got the best out of and who, like Norman had exploded onto the scene as a novice teenager with United. Brian was a big powerful player, who was difficult to knock off the ball and who would always score you a few goals into the bargain.

Chapter 15

GREAT PLAYERS OF MY ERA
From other clubs

During my Everton career, there were many players who stood out as formidable opponents and in the eyes of their own supporters were the best around. With our neighbours (unfortunately) ruling the roost during the eighties, my strongest memories are of many of the Liverpool players of that time. It is little wonder really that they won so much, when they had players of the calibre of Kenny Dalglish, Graeme Souness and Ian Rush in their side.

Kenny Dalglish

Dalglish had to be closely watched all the time, as he only required seconds to snatch at the ball and have it resting in the back of your net, while you made up your mind what to do. He was also an expert at shielding the ball from you and then setting up a team mate with a scoring opportunity. Liverpool's success owed a lot to the skill of Dalglish.

Graeme Souness

Souness on the other hand was the hard man of the side, although Jimmy Case and Steve McMahon were not to be ignored in this department. The Scot could also score his fair share of goals and it was his drive, which at times kept that particular team going.

Ian Rush

My Welsh team-mate, Ian Rush, was simply a goal machine, who required even less time than Dalglish to sniff out a goal-scoring chance. Facing the likes of Rushie every week would have been a complete nightmare and as cup draws often paired Liverpool and Everton together, I would, unfortunately, come face to face with him more than twice a season. Playing against him at least kept you on your toes, as you could never relax when up against him.

The best finisher that I have ever seen, although I have to say that I did get the better of him during the early days of our careers. Rushie is still one of my best mates, a friendship established many many years ago in the Flintshire Shoolboys under-13 team

Steve McMahon

Another former Anfield man who I had a lot of time for and one who is a really good friend, despite our on-field rivalry, is Steve McMahon. We were of course team-mates at Goodison and I remember him joining us a schoolboy, not long after I arrived at the club.

From the youth team to the reserves and into the first team we progressed together, subsequent moves saw Steve end up across the park at Anfield. Our friendship though never floundered and along with our wives, we were often in each other's company. The rivalry was simply kept for the 90 minutes out on the pitch.

So, who else stands out from around that particular time?

Liam Brady

Arsenal's Liam Brady was another tremendously gifted individual, who ruled their midfield and created a host of goal-scoring chances for his team mates. His passing, from any distance made him a player to watch, both on the field and from the stands and terracing.

Bryan Robson

Another mid-field player you couldn't ignore was Manchester United's Bryan Robson. Unlucky at times with injuries, Robbo was United's answer to Souness. Many of his injuries came about due to his total involvement in the game and would not have happened to many other players, as they would never have thrown themselves into the thick of things like Bryan did.

He was a typical captain, who led by example and a player I knew he would never consider a game lost until the final whistle. A truly inspirational player and a role model for many youngsters at that time.

UNITED REVIEW

MANCHESTER UNITED
FOOTBALL CLUB

©

TONIGHT'S MATCH SPONSORED BY Bradford & Bingley BUILDING SOCIETY BBB

MANCHESTER UNITED v EVERTON

Football League Division One, Season 1979-1980

Wednesday, 12th March 1980, kick off 7.30 p.m. Price 20p

Chapter 16

MEMORABLE GAMES
For Everton and Wales

MANCHESTER UNITED v EVERTON at Old Trafford, March 12th 1980

I made my debut under the Old Trafford lights on March 12th 1980 at the age of 19, taking over the blue number four shirt from Billy Wright. I only really got my chance due to manager Gordon Lee being somewhat restricted in his selection options, as seven members of his first-team squad were either out through injuries, illness or suspension.

The team that faced United that night showed two actual and one positional changes from the side that had defeated Ipswich Town 2-1 in the FA Cup 6th round tie four days earlier.

Up until then, Everton hadn't enjoyed the best of seasons, showing little consistency and we had picked up only two League points from the previous six fixtures prior to the game against United. We had, however, progressed to the sixth round of the FA Cup as I mentioned, and the luck of the draw was certainly with us, producing home ties against Aldershot, Wigan and Wrexham.

United at that time had the likes of Ray Wilkins, Sammy McIlroy, Arthur Albiston, Joe Jordan and Lou Macari in their side and to be honest weren't a bad side and were mounting something of a championship challenge against our neighbours Liverpool. So, I suppose the 0-0 draw was indeed a point gained, rather than one lost.

Having said that, United certainly weren't at their best that night, with sections of their support actually giving their players a bit of stick over their performance. They also had a few opportunities to snatch all the points, but failed to take them.

Our players obviously had one eye on the forthcoming semi-final against West Ham United, but because of our indifferent League performances, we could not afford to have one foot off the pedal, as there was every possibility off us slipping into the relegation zone.

As for my own performance, I was certainly nervous as we approached the stadium, with the United supporters along the way giving us a noisy 'welcome' and it took me a few early touches to settle down once the game got under way. After that, I felt quite comfortable and began to enjoy the game. Thankfully, I did not have too much to do and came through the 90 minutes without having committed any major mistakes.

Neither did I grab the following day's back page headlines, although I remember Derek Wallis of the 'Daily Mirror' writing "…with Kevin Ratcliffe making an impressive debut." That was good enough for me. I was on my way!

Above: Billy Wright.
Top centre: Martin Hodge.
Top right: West Ham's scorer on Saturday Stuart Pearson.
Right: Billy Wright.
Far right: Phil Parkes.
Below: Trevor Brooking, Stuart Pearson (West Ham), Trevor Ross (Everton) at Villa Park on Saturday.

Football Association Challenge Cup

SEMI-FINAL REPLAY

WEST HAM UNITED V EVERTON

ELLAND ROAD, LEEDS
WEDNESDAY 16th APRIL, 1980
Kick-off 7.45 p.m.

OFFICIAL SOUVENIR PROGRAMME 40p

EVERTON v WEST HAM UNITED at Elland Road, April 16th 1980
FA Cup semi-final replay

After making my debut at Old Trafford I found myself back on the sidelines until our FA Cup semi-final replay with West Ham United at Elland Road. The club hadn't been to the FA Cup Final since 1968 and hopes were high around Goodison that this could be our year. With Liverpool playing Arsenal in the other semi everyone was talking about the possibility of a first all-Merseyside final.

My inclusion in the team came as a major shock. Brian Kidd had been sent off in the first game, a 1-1 draw at Villa Park on the Saturday, and I was drafted into the squad on the Monday. Even then I didn't envisage getting the nod to play but I was delighted when Gordon Lee named in the team at centre back.

FA Cup semi-finals are nervous occasions at the best of times, never mind when you're only 19 with just one previous game under your belt but I did my best to focus on the task ahead and once the game kicked off any nerves I did have went out of the window. With over 30,000 Evertonians inside the ground it felt like a home game and we started confidently.

Within two minutes I remember we had a penalty appeal turned down after Peter Eastoe was kicked in the chest as he tried to control the ball in the Hammers area. Billy Wright then had a header nodded off the line by West Ham skipper Billy Bonds and there's no doubt we were the better team in the first half.

As you'd expect the game became more and more tense as time ticked by. The atmosphere was highly charged and I was spoken to by referee Colin Seel following a confrontation with Alan Devonshire. Both sides had a goal disallowed shortly after the break and the 90 minutes finished goalless.

Tiredness set in as we started extra-time and we fell behind shortly afterwards. Devonshire was the scorer, squeezing the ball under Martin Hodge following a neat one-two with Stuart Pearson.

West Ham may have been a Second Division side at the time but they were a good team and as their famous 'Bubbles' song bellowed around the ground our Wembley dream looked to be fading.

With seven minutes remaining however we thought we'd snatched a draw and forced another replay when Bob Latchford, with a classic chest high diving header drew us level.

The relief was palpable but as thoughts began to turn to a third game at Coventry's Highfield Road Frank Lampard unexpectedly popped up to break Evertonian hearts with a stooping header.

To quote two famous football clichés I was as sick as a parrot to have lost, especially in such cruel circumstances, but at the same time I was over the moon to have played for Everton in such a big game and I also tripled my weekly wage by getting an appearance fee!

In the dressing room afterwards people like Mike Lyons were crying, saying "You've got plenty of time to get to another final, we'll not get another chance."

They were right, my time would come.

WALES v. CZECHOSLOVAKIA

WORLD CUP QUALIFYING TIE – GROUP 3

GORAU·CHWARAE·CYD·CHWARAE

NINIAN PARK, CARDIFF
WED., 19th NOVEMBER, 1980 – KICK OFF 7.30 p.m.

OFFICIAL PROGRAMME 30p

WALES v CZECHOSLOVAKIA, November 19th 1980
My Welsh International Debut

I was drafted into the Welsh squad just before my 20th birthday and it came as something of a surprise, even though there was no glut of players to choose from, as I had only played in a handful of first-team games for Everton.

It was strange meeting up with the rest of the squad and I felt a little apprehensive as most 'new boys' would, but I was soon made welcome and settled down to enjoy the experience. I had of course been a member of the under 21 squad, so the international scene was not completely alien to me. It was just that the other players were in general experienced professionals.

Manager Mike England, the former Tottenham Hotspur centre half had told us in his pre-match team talk to be positive in anything that we did and we heeded his words early in the game. Former Manchester United, Wrexham, Chelsea and of course Everton winger Micky Thomas was putting in some fine work out on the wing and it was from one of his passes across the face of the Czech goal that left David Giles with the simple task of scoring from only six yards out after just nine minutes.

The experienced Czech side almost immediately tried to play themselves back into the game and came close to equalising after half an hour, when Dai Davies could only push out a curling cross. Nehoda connected with the loose ball, but Walsh managed to clear the impeding danger.

The passionate 20,000 Ninian Park crowd were soon being treated to an exciting end-to-end game, with neither side too concerned about their defensive responsibilities

Early in the second half, Carl Harris, on as a substitute for goalscorer Giles, almost put us two in front with a powerful drive, which ended a three-man, 60-yard move. Another opportunity came in the 66th minute, when Bryan Flynn was obstructed in the penalty area by Radimecl. The West German referee, however, simply waved away all our claims for a penalty as Walsh shot past the post with the goal begging. Perhaps the official was playing the advantage rule, but we did not gain anything from it.

Harris was to test the goalkeeper again, but there was to be no more scoring as we recorded our third consecutive World Cup qualifying win, giving us maximum points in our group.

It was something of a relief to hear the final whistle and as we reflected on the game and result back in the dressing room, it dawned on us that we had just beaten one of the best teams in the world, with a good determined effort.

In action against Germany

WALES v GERMANY, June 5th 1991
European Championship, Group 5 Qualifier

Any game against the reigning World Champions is a massive one but with Wales challenging strongly for a place in their first major tournament since 1958 the importance of this clash could not be understated.

With five points from a possible six we went into the game top of our qualifying group - one point ahead of the Germans who had a game in hand. Victory would leave qualification in our own hands and an expectant Welsh public turned out in force at Cardiff Arms Park.

The task we faced was an awesome one. Bertie Vogts' side were unbeaten in 16 games and during the first twenty minutes it looked as though we were going to be played off the park. With the likes of Lothar Matheus, Andy Brehme and Rudi Voeller stroking the ball about with ease we struggled to get a touch and Jurgen Klinsmann went close to opening the scoring following a mistake by yours truly!

Luckily my Everton team-mate Big Nev was, as ever, in fine form between the sticks and he spared my blushes with a fine save. After that scare we gradually began to force our way back into the game and could have gone in at the interval in the lead. Barry Horne crashed a shot from 35-yards against the bar and Paul Bodin had a goalward bound shot blocked.

With the German captain Matheus limping off injured at half-time we began to dominate more and more, and on the hour mark the tide really began to turn in our favour when Thomas Berthold was sent off after kicking me as I lay on the ground!

It was his second bookable offence of the night and the Belgian referee had no option but to dismiss him. With an extra man we went for the jugular and six minutes later made the crucial breakthrough we deserved.

Bodin knocked a long ball over the top of the five-man German defence. Ian Rush gave chase, brushed aside the challenge of Buchwald and in typical Rushie fashion held his nerve to coolly slot the ball past Illgner.

It was the 19th goal of his Wales career and one he later described as the most important of his international career. Germany hit back as you'd expect and lay siege to our goal in the closing stages but further heroics from Neville kept them at bay and we managed to hold on.

Great celebrations greeted the sounding of the final whistle and the victory was hailed in the press as one of Wales' greatest ever. It moved us three points clear at the top of the group, meaning a draw in the return against Germany and a win over Luxembourg in our final game would guarantee us a place in Euro 92.

But nothing is ever that straightforward when it comes Wales and qualification for the big tournaments!

Battling in the air against Belgium

WALES v BELGIUM, March 31st 1993

All good things must come to an end and the game against Belgium, marked the end of my career as a Welsh international player. Obviously at that time, I did not know this, but looking back, at least I did manage to go out with a victory.

The match itself produced two noteworthy events for the record books. Firstly, it saw the first start in the red of Wales for Manchester United prodigy Ryan Giggs. He had already featured as a substitute on five previous occasions, but that first start is always THE one.

Ryan, however, was upstaged by a certain Ian Rush, whose 24th international goal in the 39th minute broke Trevor Ford and Ivor Allchurch's previous record.

We got off to something of a bad start, with defender Eric Young booked for a bad foul for a tackle from behind on Czerniatynski, but we soon settled down to play some good football. We almost took the lead early on, when Bodin connected on to a Giggs back heel, only to be thwarted by a Belgian defender who blocked his shot.

In the 18th minute, we did open the scoring. Dean Saunders was brought down by Boffin and from the resulting free kick Giggs found the net. This was only the second goal that the Belgians had conceded in the group games.

Neville Southall had to make a couple of fine saves from Albert and Czerniatynski, to keep the visitors at bay, but we managed to hold on to our lead as the first half came to an end. This was despite the visitors having more or less dominated the play.

After the break, we kept up the momentum. Mark Hughes sent the effervescent Saunders through, but after getting the better of two defenders, he shot rather tamely into the arms of the Belgian goalkeeper. Ian Rush should also have increased his goals tally in the 52nd minute after being set up by Giggs, but the opportunity was squandered.

The score remained at 2-0 and we walked off the pitch feeling quite confident of reaching the World Cup finals in the United States. Our dreams, unfortunately never materialised and Welshmen could only watch the finals from afar and think of what might have been.

Whether or not I would have been part of the squad had we reached the finals I do not know, but as the history books show, Wales did not feature in the World Cup finals of 1994 and the name of Kevin Ratcliffe never again featured on a Welsh team sheet.

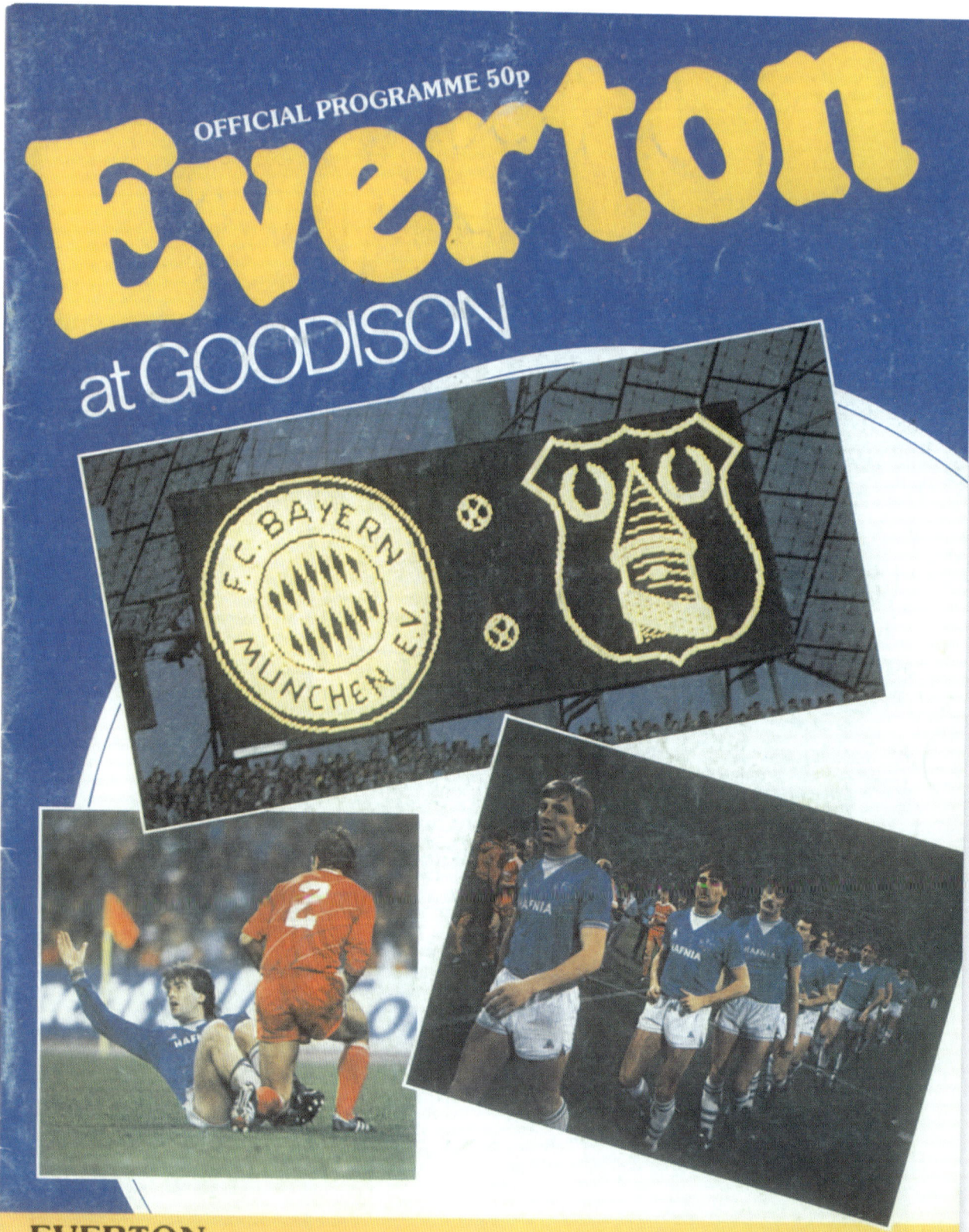

OFFICIAL PROGRAMME 50p

Everton
at GOODISON

**EVERTON v
BAYERN MUNICH**
European Cup Winners' Cup
Semi-final — 2nd Leg
Wednesday 24th April 1985

Inside Tonight's Programme . . .
**PROFILE ON NEVILLE SOUTHALL
IN COLOUR — ACTION AND NEWS
FROM THE FIRST LEG IN MUNICH**

EVERTON v BAYERN MUNICH at Goodison Park, April 24th 1985
European Cup Winners Cup, Semi-final, 2nd Leg

Ask anyone who has ever played competitive football and they will tell you that there is nothing worse than losing a cup semi-final. You have struggled through the earlier rounds and are only 90 minutes away from a Final and a possible winners medal, then defeat and you have nothing to show for your efforts.

An appearance in any final is acceptable. From the local League to the ultimate on the domestic calendar, the FA Cup. Some though get the opportunity to go onto a higher level and play in the finals of European competitions or even the World Cup. We had progressed steadily in the 1985 European Cup Winners Cup, against rather unfashionable opposition in the form of UC Dublin, Slovan Bratislava and Fortuna Sittard to reach the semi-finals, where our opponents were the rather more familiar and certainly tougher Bayern Munich.

Drawn away in the first leg, we held out for a very creditable 0-0 draw. We therefore had everything to play for in front of the Goodison Park faithful.

The Germans were clearly out to unsettle us and several early tackles ruffled a few feathers, with Graeme Sharp and Peter Reid on the receiving end more than most. Trevor Steven was a thorn in the Bayern side early on, shooting across goal when he possibly could have done better, while Kevin Sheedy forced Pfaff into a fine save. In the Bayern side, their young winger Kogl was a constant threat.

Neither team gave an inch and Andy Gray's name found its way into the referee's notebook for retaliation and soon afterwards the same player was involved in a challenge with Eder, which left the German in a heap, with blood pouring from a facial wound.

Sheedy came close on a couple of occasions before we found ourselves a goal behind. A through ball from Matthaus caught our defence flat and although big Nev managed to block Kogl's shot, the ball rebounded to Hoeness, who unhurriedly placed the ball between the two blue shirts standing on the goal line. This was the first goal that we had conceded in the competition and it was certainly not the best time to do so.

Still, the crowd raised the noise level a few decibels and the lads now knew what they had to do if they wanted a place in the final.

The Germans held out until three minutes after the interval, when it was a slip from their goalkeeper that allowed us back in the game. Pfaff dropped a long throw in from Gary Stevens, and before he could react, Graeme Sharp had prodded the ball over the line.

If the scoreline remained the same, we were out and with less than 15 minutes to go, there were many nervous looks at watches around the ground.

In the 72nd minute, Andy Gray, ideally placed in front of goal, put us 2-1 in front but the game was far from over. Frantic shouts from the bench made us realise that there was not long remaining, so we had to be extra cautious, especially at the back. However, with only four minutes left, we could at last relax and enjoy the evening, when Trevor Steven put the game beyond all doubt, running through to score our third.

History was beckoning.

My shirt from the E.C.W. Cup Final in 1985

EVERTON v RAPID VIENNA at Feyenoord Stadium, Rotterdam, May 15th 1985
European Cup Winner's Cup Final

It was only a quick jaunt across the English Channel, but when most professionals are already heading for some relaxing sunshine, we were far from relaxed following a long, hard, but victorious League campaign, as there were still two games remaining on our fixture list. Two important ones at that.

But, it was that old adage of taking one game at a time, so the European Cup Winners Cup Final against Rapid Vienna was firmly in our focus.

I have mentioned our route to the final in the previous 'Memorable Game', so it is straight into a match which could be described as the most important in the history of the club. Our opponents, Rapid Vienna, would certainly be no pushovers, as their physical approach in a controversial encounter against Celtic in a previous round was still fresh in the memory.

Howard Kendall had of course done his homework, so we all knew who was who and what to expect from the Austrians. It was time to stand up and be counted as our moment of destiny was near.

The manager was well aware that Rapid were a little bit wary regarding our aerial threat of Andy Gray and Graeme Sharp, so a route one for goal was certainly one of our plans and as it was implemented, it had a clearly unsettling effect on our opponents.

Despite our pressure, their defence managed to withstand whatever came their way, but there was no frustration within our ranks as we simply kept our heads and remembered the instructions and game plan that had been discussed in the dressing room prior to the match.

By doing so we thought that we had earned our reward six minutes before the break. Having won yet another free kick, Kevin Sheedy directed his kick high into the Rapid penalty area, where the tall figure of Derek Mountfield rose to connect with the ball, heading it into the path of Andy Gray.

Without a moments hesitation, the big Scotsman swept the ball home, but a linesman's flag brought a premature end to our celebrations, adjudging Mountfield to have been offside. At the time, we were unaware that television replays back home were showing that the goal was completely legitimate and should have stood.

Putting that minor disappointment behind us, we continued to attack, even more determined to break down the Austrian's defence.

Half time came and went, the score remaining at 0-0. Then 12 minutes after the restart the deadlock was eventually broken.

For once the Rapid defence slipped up as a back pass to goalkeeper Konsel was carelessly under-hit. Sniffing the half chance, Graeme Sharp reached the ball before the 'keeper and calmly took it round the now stranded figure. Spotting Andy Gray moving in on goal, Sharp picked out his fellow countryman with an exquisite chip and from a few yards out Andy, more or less on his own, had no problem in scoring.

Exchanging pennants with Hans Krankl (Vienna) at the kick off

Our experience carried us through the next few nervous moments as we tried to settle down after soaring to a high after the goal and as the Austrians began to press for the equaliser.

However an equaliser did not materialise, as in the 72nd minute we increased our lead. A corner from Kevin Sheedy floated through the night air and eluded floundering Rapid defenders, the ball falling at the feet of Trevor Steven at the far post. Before any defenders managed to react, Trevor had hammered the ball home. We had one hand on the trophy.

Our opponents, though, still felt that they had something to play for and that there was a possibility of clawing themselves back into the game. Their hopes were raised by a Krankl goal and our visions of collecting winner's medals momentarily blurred.

Any hopes that Rapid now harboured for an equaliser were almost immediately squashed, as we sped up field from the restart and Kevin Sheedy fired a tremendous drive into the back of the Austrians' net from what was all of 25 yards.

This time, there was no way back for Rapid and with the minutes ticking away, I knew that the trophy was to be ours.

Stretching my legs in the FA Cup Final

EVERTON v WATFORD at Wembley Stadium, May 19th 1984
FA Cup Final

They say that you need your fair share of luck to win any cup competition and I suppose when you look back, we had a little bit of that as we strode to Wembley in 1984.

We had already visited the old north London ground a couple of months earlier, to play neighbours Liverpool in the Milk Cup final. We drew that particular match 0-0, only to lose 1-0 in the Maine Road replay, so we were determined not to lift runners-up medals the second time around.

Our campaign got underway at Stoke, where Andy Gray and Alan Irvine goals gave us a 2-0 victory, but it was in the fourth round that we required our slice of cup luck.

Drawn at home to Gillingham, I think it is fair to say that the majority of our supporters expected a win, without too much trouble. To their credit, Gillingham played well and held out for a 0-0 draw, managing to repeat the performance in front of their own supporters, three days later. On either occasion we could quite easily have become the recipients of a giant killing.

A second replay eventually proved too much for the Priestfield side and two goals from Kevin Sheedy and one from Adrian Heath saw us through to face another side of a lower division in Shrewsbury Town. The Goodison Park crowd was certainly not kept on tender hooks this time as we won rather comfortably, 3-0.

Having beaten our next opponents, Notts County, 4-1 at Goodison a few weeks before, we had no fear about visiting Meadow Lane for our sixth round tie and duly won 2-1. One step from Wembley and only Southampton between us and our second final of the season.

Playing at Highbury, the South Coast club gave us a tough afternoon and at the end of the 90 minutes, it was an Adrian Heath goal that separated the two teams.

It had been some 18 years since Everton had lifted the FA Cup, with their supporters having to endure countless goadings from their red rivals during that time. Our opponents Watford, under Graham Taylor, showed plenty of enthusiasm but were no match for a team determined to end a long barren, trophyless spell.

It could, however, have been a much different outcome if John Barnes had not failed to take advantage of a long throw into our goalmouth in what was only the second minute of the game.

Play moved from end to end with both sides scorning opportunities, before we took the lead as the first half wore on. Kevin Richardson crossed into the Watford penalty area and surprisingly, their defence failed to sense any immediate danger.

Gary Stevens reacted quickest and his shot-cum-pass was stopped by Graeme Sharp before the big Scot turned and fired home, with the ball taking a slight deflection off the post.

Parading the FA Cup with Kevin Richardson

Content with our 1-0 interval lead and in no real danger from Watford, we knew that another goal would finish their aspirations and we certainly did not have long to wait for that particular moment.

With only six minutes of the second half played, Andy Gray rose alongside Watford goalkeeper Sherwood as they both went for a Trevor Steven cross. The mid-air challenge saw Andy head the ball home, as the 'keeper looked for a free kick. The goal stood, we played out the game comfortably and took the cup back to Goodison Park.

Climbing those steps at Wembley to receive the trophy is something I will never forget and it was a moment to savour.

My BBC Man-of-the-Match award from the final

Pistols at the ready between Ian Rush and myself

EVERTON v LIVERPOOL at Goodison Park, February 20th 1991

Local 'derby' matches rarely conjure up memorable encounters, but on February 20th 1991, Liverpool's short journey across Stanley Park managed to find itself remembered by both sides, for completely different reasons.

The game, was an FA Cup 5th round replay and having drawn 0-0 at Anfield three days previously we were certainly confident of progressing further at our rivals expense. Our confidence, however, was dented just after the half-hour mark when Peter Beardsley was on hand to score, after Ian Rush had a shot blocked on the line.

Two minutes after the interval, Sharp headed home a Hinchcliffe cross, but Beardsley out foxed our defence to put Liverpool back in front with 20 minutes still to play. Once again though, we managed to pull level, with something of a gift from Grobbelaar and Nicol. The two Liverpool players collided, allowing Graeme Sharp the simplest of scoring opportunities.

With play moving from end to end, Rush put Liverpool once again in front. A goal that they thought had won them a place in the next round. But, with five minutes remaining, Tony Cottee's goal pushed the game into extra time.

Yet again, Liverpool went in front, with a goal worthy of winning any game, when John Barnes screwed a 25-yard shot past my Welsh team mate in goal. It wasn't, however, going to win this particular game.

Time was running away from us and with a mere three minutes to go, Tony Cottee strode through the Liverpool defence to make the scoreline 4-4. Breathless was one way to describe it.

Talk of the game went on for days, with Kenny Dalglish's departure from the manager's office at Anfield and his retirement from professional football 48 hours later increasing the media coverage.

The second replay, unfortunately brought no repeat goal avalanche and a solitary Dave Watson strike won the game for us.

Attempting to clear the ball from Kevin Drinkell of Norwich

NORWICH v EVERTON at Carrow Road, May 4th 1987

Throughout any trophy-winning campaign, there will always be one or two games that remain in the memory and this was certainly one of them. However, I must state that for me, it wasn't just one or two games that stood out, but the overall performance of the team, particularly over the testing Christmas period.

Taking full points from the four holiday fixtures became even more important when none of our rivals managed to do likewise. But a slight dip in form following our FA Cup defeat by Wimbledon took us four games to get back on course.

Slowly we clawed ourselves back into the thick of things and with three games remaining, the destination of the Championship was decided.

We journeyed to East Anglia, knowing that a victory against Norwich City would be enough to give us the title, and it was achieved with none of the flair that we had previously shown, but by pure hard graft and determination.

With less than one minute played we took the lead through the unusual source of defender Pat Van den Hauwe.

Knowing what victory would bring us, it was perhaps not the best time to score, as it meant that we had to walk a nervous tightrope for the remaining 89 minutes. But, hold on we did and the victory itself was rather more notable due to the fact that Norwich City had only lost once at home in the league during that season.

Our supporters were loud in their acclaim of the title, with the result, for once, being more important than the manner in which it was achieved. Football should always be entertaining, but when so much depends on the result then those ideas sometimes have to be abandoned.

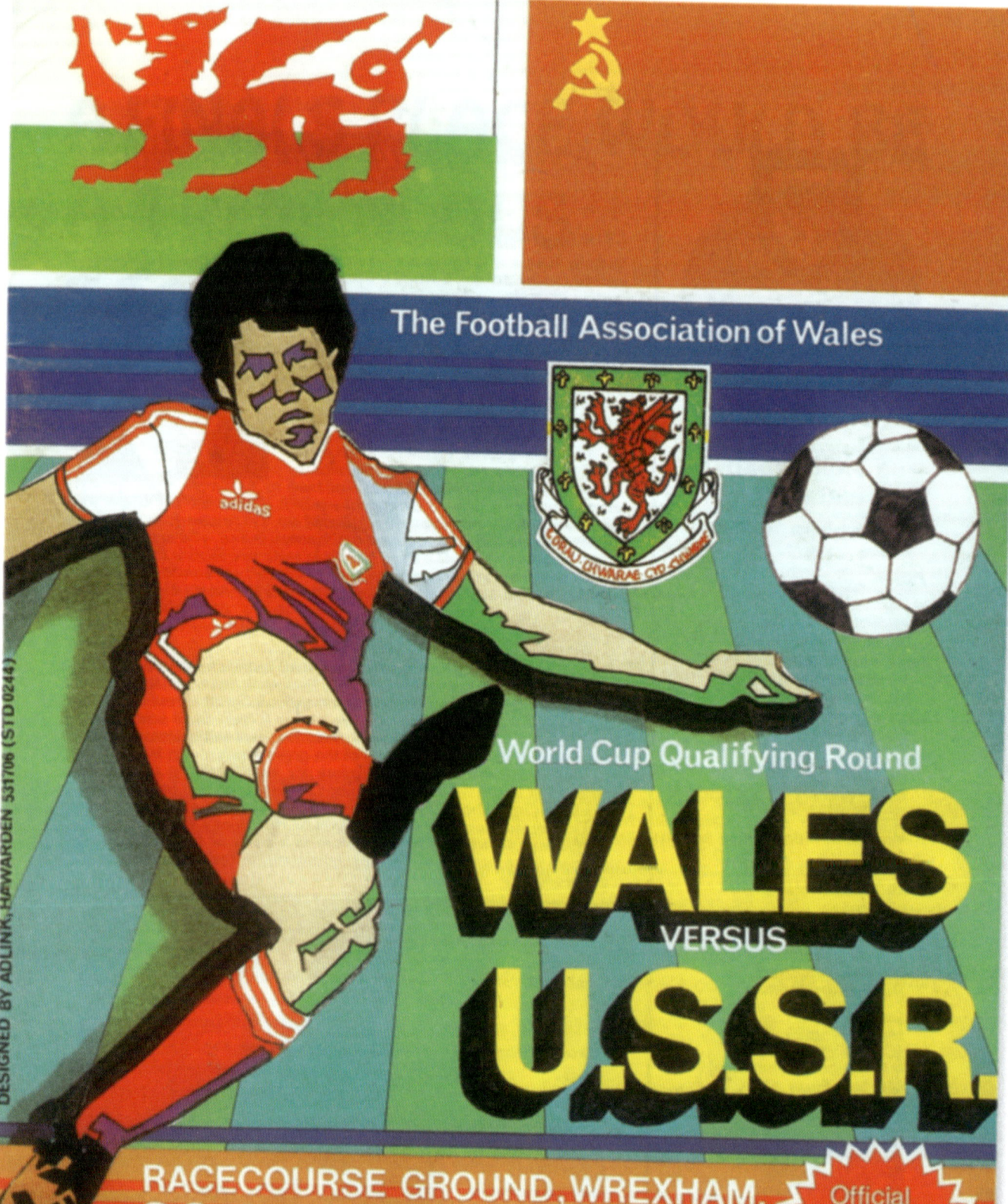

The Football Association of Wales

World Cup Qualifying Round

WALES
VERSUS
U.S.S.R.

RACECOURSE GROUND, WREXHAM.
30th May 1981. KICK OFF 3 P.M.

Official Programme 40p

DESIGNED BY ADLINK, HAWARDEN 531706 (STD 0244)

Chapter 17

FIRE BREATHING DRAGONS
Highlights of my International Career

WALES v USSR at The Racecourse Ground, May 30th 1981

After performing favourably in our last three internationals, drawing 0-0 with England at Wembley, beating Scotland 2-0 in Swansea and gaining a notable 1-0 World Cup group qualifier success over Turkey in Ankara's quaintly named 19 May Stadium, we were quietly confident that we could get a favourable result against the Soviet Union.

It was imperative that we gained something from the World Cup group three qualifier against the favourites, if we were going to have any hopes of going to Spain the following summer. If we could beat the USSR, we would then only have to defeat Iceland to book our flights.

Wrexham's compact Racecourse Ground was packed for the game and no one underestimated the Soviets, with the likes of Baltacha, Bessonov and Blokhin always likely to cause problems. Indeed, a cross from the latter in the seventh minute was fortunately missed by Kipiani.

Although our limited resources were something of a handicap at times, we gave our physically superior visitors a hard time, with tenacious tackling and strong running.

I remember having something of a nervous start due to the importance of the fixture, but soon settled down.

We might have fared slightly better if Leighton James had been fit, but as it was, our creative openings were really few and far between.

In the second half, Dai Davis made a couple of really excellent first-class saves from Oganisian, while I set up a good scoring opportunity for Walsh, but he could not control the ball.

As it was, the game fizzled out with the result goalless, giving us therefore a fighting chance of qualifying. There was, however, to be disappointment on the horizon.

Wales and England shirts

WALES v ENGLAND at The Racecourse Ground, May 2nd 1984

This was not just any old international fixture, it was the last Home International meeting between the two countries. The final encounter of 90 games that had stretched over a 105-year period.

Our team, as was often the case, lacked the experience of our English opponents. But what we lacked in that department, we more than made up for in determination and vigour, as we were desperate to prove a point to the visiting officials who felt that such fixtures did not matter.

The game was still settling down, when we gave England something of a jolt by opening the scoring in the 17th minute. A goal that was in fact, to decide the outcome of the match and it came from the Manchester United combination of Mark Hughes and Alan Davies.

Mark Wright, showing debut nerves, brought down Ian Rush and taking the free kick, Davies swung it towards the opposition goal, where Hughes out jumped the England defence to head past Peter Shilton. A debutant who showed no sign of nerves.

England, to be honest, rarely threatened us and it wasn't until seven minutes into the second half that we were put under any sort of pressure. Even then, Alvin Martin's header was pushed on to the crossbar by Southall and Micky Thomas cleared off the line.

They were not to cause any further problems and we stood firm as the game fizzled out.

It was a game that we really had to win following all the pre-match hype relating to it being the last fixture between the two countries for the foreseeable future. The Welsh media giving the impression that England felt that we were not good enough to play against. I suppose that is just what the powers that be did think. We were happy to cause them some embarassment.

Shaking hands with Spain captain Luis Arconada before the match

WALES v SPAIN at The Racecourse Ground, April 30th 1985

As a player, manager and of course spectator, I have witnessed hundreds, or perhaps thousands, of goals being scored. Not too many of them by myself though. Some of those have been creditable efforts, while others have been nothing short of flukes.

Watching from the stands or terraces, you get a better view of most of these at the game you are attending. But, on the evening of April 30th 1985, I witnessed one of the best goals I have ever seen and it would have mattered little if I had seen it from the terraces, stands or even on television, it would have looked no better than it did a few yards down the pitch from me.

Wales were playing host to Spain in a World Cup group seven qualifier at Wrexham. A match which saw us trounce the visitors 3-0.

It was a hard fought 90 minutes, with the Spaniards employing Maceda as a sweeper, in order to try and contain Ian Rush along with a hatchet man, Goicoechea to give Mark Hughes a hard time. By the end of the game, both the visiting players were totally frustrated.

Although we won 3-0, one of the goals was worth the admission money alone and as I said earlier, one of the best I have ever seen.

In the 53rd minute, Peter Nicholas sent a free kick into the Spaniards penalty area and a challenge from Mickey Thomas saw the ball bounce back towards Mark Hughes.

The ball bounced rather awkwardly, waist high, in front of Mark, he suddenly launched himself some three feet off the ground and while almost horizontal, volleyed the ball with his right foot high into the Spanish goal, past the helpless Arconada.

I can still see it today, one of the highlights of my playing career never mind my international career.

Forcing Belgium's Marc DeGryce into hurrying his shot

WALES v BELGIUM October 17th 1990
European Championship Group 5 Qualifier

This was the game in which I chalked up my half century of international appearances and as you can imagine it was one of the proudest moments of my career.

When I won my first senior cap for Wales little did I think that one day I would emulate the feat of some legendary Welsh footballers. Only eleven players had previously done likewise and to take my place alongside such revered names as Ivor Allchurch, Dai Davies, Brian Flynn and Terry Yorath was a big thrill.

Belgium were the opposition at Cardiff Park Arms Park as we embarked on the road to what he hoped would lead to the Euro 92 finals in Sweden and it was by no means the easiest game to open our qualifying campaign.

Despite losing to England at the second round stage of the World Cup just a few months previous the Belgians were renowned as one of the continents top sides. Their record over the past decade more than proved that. For such a small country the success they'd achieved was nothing short of remarkable and an inspiration to all similar sized nations, including Wales. In 1980 they'd gone all the way to the final of the European Championship and six years later reached the last four of the World Cup in Mexico.

Their team was in something of a transitional phase however and they weren't considered to be the force they once were. Nevertheless with the likes of Eric Gerets, Jan Ceulemans, Enzo Scifo and Francois Van der Elst in their starting line-up they still represented formidable opposition.

As for ourselves, having scored just five goals in our last nine outings we went into the game low on confidence and considering the fact that we could boast a strike force of Rush, Hughes and Saunders – one that would be the envy of most international sides – it had been a particularly frustrating spell.

Our confidence was dented further when Bruno Versavel fired Belgium into the lead after 24minutes. The majority of the 15,000 crowd were stunned and must have been fearing the worst but within five minutes we were level. Dean Saunders split the Belgian defence with a perfectly threaded through ball and Rushie ran through to notch his first international goal in 28 months.

It was a strike that seemed to have a galvanizing effect on us and we went on to bombard the Belgian goal after the break, only to be denied time and again by the heroics of keeper Preud'homme.

It looked as though we were going to have to settle for a draw until the 82nd minute when Deano chested down a cross from Barry Horne and hammered the ball into the back of the net. Three minutes from time Mark Hughes sealed victory with an incisive finish after charging through the opposition defence.

Our strikers were back on form and what would be another exciting qualifying campaign was up and running. It was an impressive result and a memorable way to mark my 50th appearance for Wales.

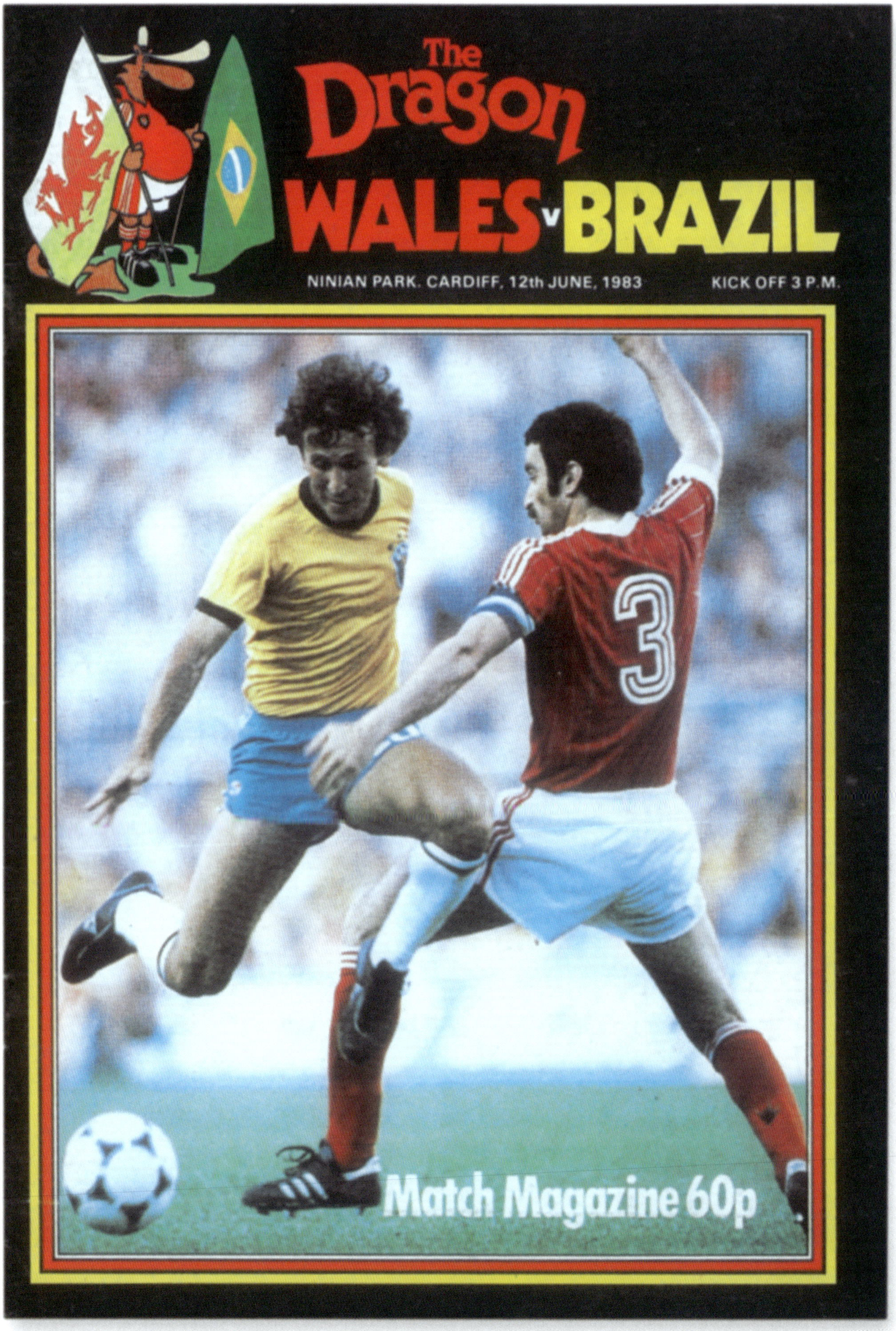

The Dragon

WALES v BRAZIL

NINIAN PARK. CARDIFF, 12th JUNE, 1983   KICK OFF 3 P.M.

Match Magazine 60p

WALES v BRAZIL at Ninian Park, June 12th 1983

The 1982/83 season had ended on a low note with Everton just missing out on European qualification but within a few weeks I was able to put that disappointment behind me when I lined up against some of the legendary Brazil team that had lit up the World Cup in Spain twelve months earlier.

This prestigious friendly had been arranged as part of Brazil's European tour and although some of their renowned squad were missing the omens for us were not good when they kicked off with a thumping 4-0 success over Portugal.

Not many pundits gave us a chance. The hot sunny weather in Cardiff that day certainly favoured the team in gold and our cause was not helped by the fact we were missing influential midfielder Peter Nicholas and prolific striker Ian Rush.

But we gave the famous Samba stars an almighty scare before a full house at Ninnian Park. The game was only four minutes old when Brian Flynn, the smallest man on the pitch, headed us into a shock lead. I don't know what the biggest surprise – Wales going a goal up against Brazil or Flynny scoring with a header!

The move that led to the goal began with Fulham striker Gordon Davies who disposed Brazil full-back Marcio out on the left. David Giles then took possession and from his cross an unmarked Flynn converted with a powerful header that nestled sweetly into the roof of the net.

For the next 57 minutes one of the biggest football upsets of all-time looked on the cards but the three time world champions hit back with a rather fortunate equalizer shortly after the hour mark.

I say fortunate because it was our failure to clear a Brazil attack that allowed them to draw level and salvage some pride. In stretching to make a tackle Jeremy Charles pulled his groin and as he lay prostrate on the ground Batista whipped in a cross which our captain for the day Joey Jones misjudged and the ball fell invitingly to the feet of Isidoro.

With just Neville Southall to beat, Isidoro, on as a half-time substitute for Pita, made no mistake. It was not the type of magical goal you'd normally associate with the great Brazil teams of the past but it was enough to make it 1-1 and that was the end of the scoring.

Still, drawing with Brazil was no disgrace. It was a result that helped put Welsh football back on the map and it had been a great thrill to pit my wits against some of the world's best players.

Everton's next 'White Pele' I may not have become – after all there is only Colin Harvey! – but I like to think I learned a lot from playing against Brazil that afternoon.

With Scotland Captain Willie Miller before the game

WALES v SCOTLAND at Ninian Park, September 10th 1985

The Welsh media clearly raised the tension for this game with their pre-match build up, seeking revenge for the defeat at the hands of Scotland in 1977 when Joe Jordan's handball decided the outcome of that match.

For something of a change, it was Scotland who were fielding the more inexperienced team, with only 181 international caps compared with our 302. We had even scored more goals than they had, or I should say that Ian Rush had.

From the offset, Mark Hughes set about the Scottish defence like a man possessed, causing the Aberdeen pairing of McLeish and Miller all sorts of problems and it was the Manchester United man who was to break the deadlock.

On the left, Peter Nicholas collected a throw in and moved past Aitken and Nicol without much of a problem. His low cross was deadly accurate for the on-running Hughsie, who shot home through the legs of Willie Miller. Needless to say, the crowd went absolutely ballistic.

I remember some hilarity in our dressing room during the half-time interval, when we were told that the Scots were replacing Jim Leighton in goal as he had lost a contact lens. I wonder if he claimed that he was partly unsighted for our goal?

Anyway, the match continued to go our way in the second half, and it began to look as though we would claim a very important victory. Nine minutes from the end, however, our hopes suffered a severe blow.

A rather hopeful cross from Speedie hit Phillips on the arm and to our utter amazement, the referee awarded a penalty. Harsh does not describe it!

In the red hot cauldron of Ninian Park, Davie Cooper kept his cool and hit the spot kick past Neville Southall, although my big mate did get his hand to the ball.

The game ended at 1-1, but the result was soon to become immaterial, as we were told as we changed in the dressing room that Jock Stein, the Scotland manager had collapsed and died of a heart attack as the game neared the end. It was a tragedy that affected everyone present at that time and was a very sad occasion indeed.

*Being tracked by Graeme Souness
during the Scotland game at Hampden park*

SCOTLAND v WALES at Hampden Park, March 27th 1985

Rather surprisingly, Wales had not won an international match at Hampden Park since 1951 and had not scored more than one goal there since 1967. Not records to bring up in conversation never mind admit to.

This match, however, was not some Home International fixture where pride was perhaps the only thing at stake. It was a World Cup group qualifier and only an outright win would keep our hopes of qualifying alive. Going by the record books, no-one would have given us much hope and more than a few Scotsmen would probably have told us that we would have more chance of seeing a wild haggis than obtaining the result that we sought.

A defeat in Iceland had not helped our chances and our team selection for this fixture was also hampered, as we had to play a Third Division reserve centre half.

The first 45 minutes were rather poor to be honest, with very few scoring opportunities created. One did come our way though and fortunately it fell to Ian Rush.

Alex McLeish attempted to head clear in the Scottish penalty area, but collided with Mark Hughes, and the ball fell towards Ian Rush. With the home defence looking for a free kick, which never came, Ian struck the ball on the half volley and it flew past the helpless Jim Leighton. McLeish could perhaps have felt a little aggrieved, as I would have expected a free kick in similar circumstances.

Nevertheless, the goal stood and we were certainly not going to complain.

The second half saw Scotland come more into the game, but despite our rather inexperienced defence we held firm, as they failed to turn their hard work into goals.

One incident that stands out from that backs-to-the-wall second half was a high, two-footed lunge by Graeme Souness on Peter Nicholas. It was without a doubt, a sending-off offence, but to the surprise of everyone in the 62,444 crowd and the players on the pitch, even the perpetrator himself I would imagine, the referee thought not.

Chapter 18

MANAGERS
The men I've played for

Gordon Lee

Gordon Lee's arrival at Goodison came at a time when we clearly needy something of a lift and he came with the reputation of someone who could get the best out of his players.

As a player, though, he was one of those who achieved little, but as a manager he could be considered an asset to those that he served.

Even though he was given the sack by Everton, he deserves some credit for the work that he did during his three-and-a-half years there and during that time, he certainly had the club's interests at heart all the time.

I will always be grateful to him for giving me my break and I suppose in one way or another, he laid something of the foundations for the success that we were to enjoy after his departure.

As a person, I certainly liked the man, however, at the same time, he was one of those people that you knew but didn't really know.

Howard Kendall

Howard was one of my schoolboy heroes throughout his time at Everton and we enjoyed a very fruitful manager/captain relationship.

He was certainly a player's manager and was always close to us, shielding us from any pressure that might have had an adverse affect on our game, although quite prepared to take any flak directed at himself.

His transfer dealings, especially in the early days received a bit of criticism, but he eventually got together what he wanted, buying and selling quite shrewdly in order to put together a useful team.

Strangely, my career at Everton under Howard might never have materialised, as he had tried to sign me when he was manager of Blackburn Rovers. Everton had shown an interest in one of Blackburn's forwards, a player by the name of Kevin Stonehouse and Howard went as far as to suggest that a player exchange might be possible if he could have me. At that time, I would probably have gone to Ewood Park, but in hindsight, I am more than grateful that the move never materialised.

As a former Everton player, Howard was an ideal choice as manager, as he was as keen for the club to be successful as anyone. On the day of his arrival, he got us all together and made his plans, ideas and objectives quite clear. We all quite clearly shared his ambitions and this was one of the major reasons of our success during the eighties.

It came as something of a shock to everyone connected with the club in 1987, when Howard, by far Everton's most successful manager, announced that he was quitting to take over the reigns at Athletico Bilbao. He had turned down the challenge of European football once before and did not want to let the opportunity pass him by again.

Two years in Spain, was followed by a return to English football with Manchester City, where he established something of a 'Goodison Park old boys colony'. Keeping them in the top flight saw his esteem rise a little in the Moss Side area of Manchester, but he was to return to where his heart lay less than a year later.

"With Manchester City it was a love affair, but with Everton it is a marriage" he was to say and his return saw the threat of relegation quickly dispelled. Success, however did not follow second time around.

Colin Harvey

Yet another individual with "Everton" running through him like a stick of Blackpool rock.

After being forced to give up the playing side of the game whilst a Sheffield Wednesday player in 1976, Colin returned to Everton to work with the youth team. His dedication and hard work was later to see him progress to first-team coach and then manager.

To say that Colin played a big part in my Everton career is something of an understatement. After joining the club, I was to find out that Colin had actually been to watch me play for the Welsh Schoolboys side and as a member of his FA Youth Cup side, he coached me in the basics of the professional game.

Following his elevation to first-team coach, his hard edge always brought the best out of not just myself, but the rest of the players and he always demanded nothing but the best. This move by the Everton board was in my opinion something of a master stroke and played a major part in our success.

Colin is and rightly so, an Everton legend. He must however, hold something of a record as the strangest sacking in any club's history. Ten weeks into the 1990-91 season, he was dismissed by the board from his post as manager at Goodison, only to be reinstated as assistant manager six days later with the re-appointment of Howard Kendall.

Mike England

Mike had a thankless job as manager of Wales, often having to rely on Second and Third Division players to boost his squad to the required numbers. His selections, at times, did not please everyone and I reckon that he deserved much more respect and praise than he got.

He gave me my international debut, so obviously I would be expected to say nice things about him, but I honestly have a great deal of time for Mike and have often enjoyed passing countless hours discussing the ins and outs of the game.

We have gone a long way from him being the manager and me being simply one of his players, to becoming very good friends.

There have of course been other managers under whom I have played at both League and international level. Men such as Terry Yorath with Wales, Mike Pejic at Chester, Roy McFarland at Derby County, Frank Clarke at Nottingham Forest, Eddie May at Cardiff and Simon Stainrod at Dundee. From all of them I have learned something and I hope that as a player, I did not cause them too many problems and at times maybe made their job a little easier.

Chapter 19

TODAY'S GREAT PLAYERS
at Goodison Park

Wayne Rooney

Football was always better in your day, whether you are an older supporter or a retired player. Everything was better, at least in your eyes, and of course bias never comes into it. But, putting everything aside, I think that it is safe to say that the Everton of my days would wipe the floor with the current side, with no disrespect to David Moyes' team.

So, who in the current side would perhaps make it into the team I played in?

Not a difficult question to answer really, as there is only one name that would make it on to the team sheet – Wayne Rooney.

He still has a lot to prove, but he has the potential to go on to be the greatest Everton player ever. It is a big order for the youngster to emulate the likes of Dixie Dean, Alan Ball, Ray Wilson etc. etc., but if he puts his mind to it and listens to those who know about the pit falls, he can become a legend with both Everton and England.

Pity he isn't Welsh!

Chapter 20

MY ALL TIME HERO
Alan Ball

There is no problem in selecting my all time hero. There was only one player it could be – Alan Ball, the ginger haired, effervescent midfield player who was even more easily identifiable through his trademark white boots.

I can remember him being signed from Blackpool, who were a big club in those days, and England's World Cup win was made all the more tolerable due to Alan's involvement.

The record fee of £110,000 paid for Alan by Harry Catterick was certainly money well spent and the non-stop running and all-round involvement soon made him a big favourite with not just myself but all the Everton supporters. It also played a huge part in Everton's League Championship win in 1969-70.

Like the rest of the Everton fans, I was devastated when the news was released that Alan had been sold to Arsenal after a couple of hundred games in the blue jersey. It is true, the club received £220,000 for him, 100 percent profit, but they lost an important member of the team.

Over the years, I have been privileged to meet Alan on a few occasions and like anyone else, the first time felt really strange, coming face-to-face with someone who you admired and had previously only seen from a distance.

It is a great pity that Everton could not have had a few Alan Balls in more recent times, as they would surely have enjoyed their share of success.

My framed 'Roll of Honour' Certificate from Everton

The
Directors Management and Staff of
Everton Football Club
hereby place on record their appreciation of

Kevin Ratcliffe's

loyal service over a period of 15 years (1977-92)

An outstanding defender and inspirational
leader, he takes his place in the Hall of Fame at
Goodison Park
as the most successful captain in the club's
history and also the first Everton player
to make 50 full international appearances

Roll of Honour

Captain of the following Everton Teams.

Football League Champions 1984-85 and 1986-87, F.A. Cup Winners 1983-84,
European Cup-winners" Cup Winners, 1984-85   Appearances
For Everton, Three Hundred and Fifty-Nine games, Two goals in Football League

One Hundred and Thirty-Three games in Cup Competitions

For Wales, Fifty-Eight games.

R. Porter Bluecoat Chambers   August 1992

NIL SATIS

NISI OPTIMUM

MY CAREER RECORD
For Everton and Wales

- **Name:**   Kevin Ratcliffe
- **Born:**   Mancot, Flintshire, 12 November 1960
- **Position:** Defender
- **Height:**   5ft 11ins
- **Weight:**   12st 7lbs

Career

- Deeside Primary & Shotton Comprehensive Schools, Deeside Primary XI, Flint Under-13's, Flint Under-15's, Everton (apprentice, June 1977, professional November 1978), Dundee (June 1991), Everton (non-contract, October 1992), Cardiff City (free-transfer, August 1993), Nottingham Forest (non-contract, December 1993), Derby County (free-transfer, January 1994), Chester City (free-transfer, July 1994, player-manager, April 1995, retired as a player August 1996), Shrewsbury Town (manager, November 1999).

Club Honours (Everton)

- League Division One champions 1985 & 1987
- Charity Shield winners 1984, 1985 & 1987, shared 1986
- FA Cup winners 1984, runners-up 1985, 1986 & 1989
- League Cup runners-up 1984
- European Cup-winners Cup winners 1985
- Screen Sport Super Cup runners-up 1986
- Simod Cup runners-up 1988
- Zenith Data Systems Cup runners-up 1991

International/Representative Honours (Wales)

- 59 full caps, 2 Under-21 caps, 4 Youth caps.

Club Record (Everton)

Season	League	Goals	F A Cup	League Cup
1979-80	2	-	1	-
1980-81	20 (+1)	-	5	2
1981-82	25	-	1	1
1982-83	29	1	5	3
1983-84	38	-	8	11
1984-85	40	-	7	4
1885-86	39	1	5	5
1986-87	42	-	3	5
1987-88	24	-	1	4
1988-89	30	-	8	4
1989-90	24	-	7	2
1990-91	35 (+1)	-	6	3
1991-92	8 (+1)	-	-	2
Total	**356 (+3)**	**2**	**57**	**46**

My Everton testimonial shirt from 1989

Full International Matches:
- 59 caps (1 with Cardiff)

(With Everton)
- 1981 v. Czechoslovakia, Republic of Ireland, Turkey, Scotland, England, USSR.
- 1982 v. Czechoslovakia, Iceland, USSR, Spain, England.
- 1983 v. Yugoslavia, England, Bulgaria, Scotland, Northern Ireland, Brazil.
- 1984 v. Norway, Romania, Bulgaria, Yugoslavia, Scotland, England, Northern Ireland, Norway, Israel.
- 1985 v. Iceland (2), Spain (2), Norway, Scotland.
- 1986 v. Scotland, Hungary, Saudi Arabia, Uruguay
- 1987 v. Finland (2), USSR, Czechoslovakia.
- 1988 v. Denmark (2), Czechoslovakia.
- 1989 v. Finland, Israel, Sweden, West Germany.
- 1990 v. Finland, Belgium.
- 1991 v. Denmark, Belgium, Luxembourg, Republic of Ireland, Iceland, Poland, Germany.
- 1992 v. Brazil, Germany

(With Cardiff)
- 1993 v. Belgium

Under 21 Caps (With Everton): 3
- 1980 v. Holland
- 1982 v. France (2)

Fact File:
- Kevin made his Football League debut for Everton against Manchester United in March 1980 before a crowd of 45,515 at Old Trafford (0-0 draw).
- Almost left Goodison Park for Ipswich Town in 1981 (after being transfer listed).
- Took over as Everton captain in December 1983.
- Groin injury followed by a hernia operation ruled him out for 10 months in 1988.
- Everton's most successful captain of all-time, leading the club to League, FA Cup, European Cup-winners Cup and FA Charity Shield glory in the mid-1980's.
- In April 1989, received a testimonial match: Everton v. Athletico Bilbao (managed at the time by Howard Kendall, Kevin's former boss at Goodison Park).
- Played his 547th and last game at club level for Chester City v. Huddersfield Town (away) on 11 March 1995 (League Division 2).

An Everton First Division Champions 1986-87 collector's cup